Understanding Death and Illness and What They Teach About Life

An Interactive Guide for Individuals with Autism or Asperger's and their Loved Ones

CATHERINE FAHERTY

Understanding Death and Illness and What They Teach About Life

All marketing and publishing rights guaranteed to and reserved by

721 W. Abram Street
Arlington, Texas 76013
800-489-0727
817-277-0727
817-277-2270 (fax)
E-mail: info@FHautism.com
www.FHautism.com

Printed in the United States of America.

ISBN: 978-1-932565-56-0

Live as if you were to die tomorrow.
Learn as if you were to live forever.

Mahatma Gandhi

And in the end,
it's not the years in your life that count.
It's the life in your years.

Abraham Lincoln

This book is dedicated to the memories of those who have passed on from September 14, 2005 to September 14, 2006, including:

Nicholas Collins • *1920-2005*
Martha Fraley • *1918-2005*
Russell Love • *1937-2005*
Diane Cady • *1952-2006*
Bessie Parks • *1920-2006*
Eric Schopler • *1927-2006*
Sara Handlan • *1955-2006*
Meta Bowers-Racine • *1986-2006*

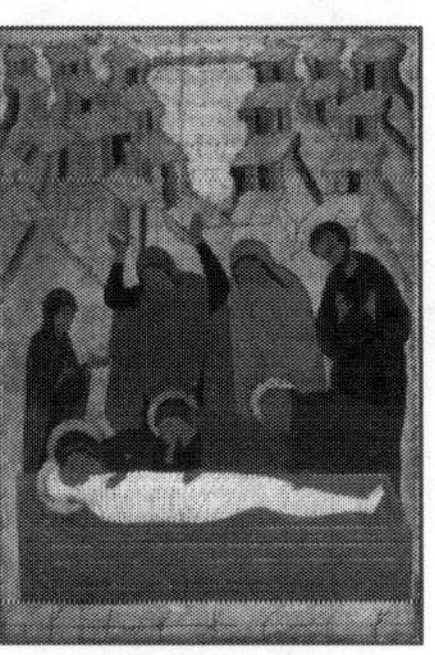

Russian Icon
Novgorod School, XVth c.

May their memories be eternal.
Αιωνια αυτων η μνημη!
Greek memorial chant.

Table of Contents

Foreword

Over the past 65 years, since Leo Kanner first described eleven youngsters in his seminal work presenting autism to the world, enormous progress has been made. Although there is still a long way to go, people with Autism Spectrum Disorders (ASD) are gaining more and more skills, leading richer lives, and successfully managing many more of the everyday challenges that face each of us in our complex society. The old image of people rocking in a custodial setting is being replaced by students learning in school, mixing with their peers, and participating in the everyday life of their community.

The progress that this represents and the advances we are seeing are very exciting to those of us who have been in this field long enough to remember the custodial institutions. The advances are truly astounding, and parents and professionals should take pride in what has been accomplished.

Although there are many reasons to rejoice, and successes to celebrate, there is still a long way to go. However, our progress has also brought new challenges to confront. Sixty years ago, no one would have thought that many people with ASD would be in a position to understand enough about the death of a family member or peer so that it would be necessary for us to explain the situation and the concepts associated with it. Today we have progressed far enough that this is one of the many challenges that confronts parents and professionals. Until now, we were pretty much on our own, relying on instinct, related experiences, and anecdotes from colleagues or friends. Thanks to this book and the courage of Catherine Faherty, who has confronted this problem and focused her energy and considerable talents on the issue over the past few years, we now have a wonderful resource to guide and support our efforts.

When Catherine first told me about this project, I was a bit overwhelmed. After all, death is something that virtually everyone struggles with at some point, and is the kind of abstract, conceptual, and non-tangible aspect of our world that people with ASD find especially troubling. How in the world, I wondered, could anyone write a book that could address death in an autism-friendly way?

How in the world, I wondered, could anyone write a book that could address death in an autism-friendly way?

As I thought a bit more about it, I understood the importance of the project because an increasing number of my clients and their families are facing the death of a relative, loved one, or friend, where a person with ASD has been involved with this process and sharing the grief. It also occurred to me that if anyone could do this project, it had to be someone with an extraordinary understanding of ASD, and remarkable talent and creativity. Of course, the person for this project had to be Catherine Faherty, and what you see is the result of her searching and incredible dedication.

The book tackles the extraordinary challenges death presents to people with ASD in a most creative and productive way...it breaks down a very abstract and diffuse concept like death into concrete and manageable components.

The book tackles the extraordinary challenges death presents to people with ASD in a most creative and productive way. It does what Catherine has always done so well: it breaks down a very abstract and diffuse concept like death into concrete and manageable components.

The book starts by explaining, in a concrete and specific way, the terms and concepts related to death. These terms allow people with ASD to understand the basic ideas and vocabulary because, in Catherine's words, "it is imperative to communicate most clearly about the things that are the most difficult to understand." It also describes and defines many of the activities and specific rituals and objects one encounters, such as funeral services, graveside services, caskets, shrouds, and other details that people with ASD will notice but might not understand. Catherine focuses on questions that are likely to relate directly to clients' experiences and concerns, like what an illness is and whether Asperger's is an illness. The book is rich with specific examples of things one can do to help with different aspects of these questions and concerns. Catherine also adds some helpful suggestions about how to handle oneself in these situations and what to do to increase your chances of living a fuller and richer life. Interesting quotes that might help a person to better understand life and death are a great bonus, and the section on expressions using the word "dead" that do not literally mean it might be especially helpful for those with ASD who often struggle with multiple meanings.

The information in this book is presented in the clear, straightforward, and concrete manner that is most likely to help those on the spectrum, as well as professionals, family members, and friends.

All in all, the result is a very full, rich, and constructive book about one of life's very difficult realities that all of us struggle with, and no one more than those with ASD. In this book, you will find a comprehensive treatment of death focusing on things most likely to concern those with ASD. The information in this book is presented in the clear, straightforward, and concrete manner that is most likely to help those on the spectrum, as well as professionals, family members, and friends. All readers of this book will learn about themselves, as well as the topic of death, and how to help people with ASD better understand and cope with it.

After reading this book, my admiration for the author, Catherine Faherty, continues to grow, along with my appreciation for her courage and conviction in making this available for all of us who care about helping people with ASD succeed in understanding this confusing and anxiety-provoking aspect of our everyday lives.

Gary B. Mesibov, Ph.D.
Professor & Director
Division TEACCH
University of North Carolina at Chapel Hill

A Mother's Essay

by Susie Heaton

Where is Mr. Paul?

There are blessings to being a parent of an ASD child. First on that list are the very special people who come into your life to help you along the path. We call ours "Wesley's Angels." Some touch our lives for just a moment, but others come and live in our hearts and lives forever. One of those angels was Mr. Paul.

We could have just never told him that Mr. Paul died. We chose not to do that. By telling Wesley, we knew we would be opening the door to questions ....

Mr. Paul was a special education bus driver in Asheville, North Carolina; Wesley was a little guy beginning elementary school. As fate would have it, Wesley was the only child on his route from our home to school and back, about a thirty-minute trip one way.

Mr. Paul was firm yet kind. Wesley would calm down just being in his presence. Some mornings Wesley would not want to go to school and would not walk to the bus. Mr. Paul would turn off the bus and get down to Wesley's level and talk to him. Sometimes he would lift him up and carry him to the bus. There was never a time that Wesley would not go with Mr. Paul. In the afternoons Mr. Paul would pull into the driveway and park the bus. He would get Wesley up on his lap and let him push buttons and, sometimes, the windshield washer and wipers and lights and bells and horn would all be going off at the same time. This was a time of joy for Wesley, Mr. Paul, and me. Every morning the bus would leave and I would hop in my car to go to work. Somewhere down the highway I would catch up with the bus and Mr. Paul would flash his lights and he and Wesley would wave at me. Sounds sort of stupid, but I felt such incredible love for this man holding my son under his protective, loving wing. Every single day Wesley would wave to Mr. Paul as he drove that little bus down our hill.

He began his new mantra, "Where is Mr. Paul?" He said it often and at unexepected times. We knew it was causing him a considerable amount of anxiety. It was causing us anxiety also, just hearing those four words over and over again.

Then we had to move. We had to go to Iowa and leave all of our friends and support in North Carolina. Several months after our move we got the news: Mr. Paul had cancer, very aggressive, and there wasn't much time. Mr. Paul left us before we could get back home for a visit.

Wesley had just turned eight years old. We could have just never told him that Mr. Paul died. We chose not to do that. By telling Wesley, we knew we would be opening the door to questions, but they were questions that would come up eventually with our own family members. You can't hide death; it is part of life.

We fumbled through telling Wesley. It is hard to explain death to any child, but an ASD child is even more difficult. They need to have a concrete answer, and there is none. We said "Mr. Paul is in heaven." He would respond, "Where is heaven?" He began his new mantra, "Where is Mr. Paul?" He said it often and at unexpected times. We knew he was obsessing over it, and it was causing him a considerable amount of anxiety. It was causing us anxiety also, just hearing those four words over and over again.

Not everyone agreed with our decision to take Wesley to the cemetery. I think that comes from our society's inability to look at death. We want to pretend it's not there. We shouldn't expose our children to it. We stuck to our gut instinct and went.

Finally, we were planning a trip home, and I decided we would take Wesley to the cemetery to show him where Mr. Paul was. I contacted Mr. Paul's wife and told her our dilemma and she told me the location of the mausoleum. She also told me that Mr. Paul had a photograph of Wesley on top of his television set up to the very end. That special love and bond never died!

Not everyone agreed with our decision to take Wesley to the cemetery. I think that comes from our society's inability to look at death. We want to pretend it is not there. We shouldn't expose our children to it. We stuck to our gut instinct and went.

It ended up being a very special, spiritual, healing day. It was a beautiful day with a Carolina blue sky. We went into the quiet mausoleum and found Mr. Paul's name on the wall. It was at Wesley's level and he could touch the name Paul Morgan and he could touch the dates, the date of birth and the date of death. He stood there and placed his hands on those letters and numbers and it was as though the understanding came. Maybe Mr. Paul was there; I don't know, but it was miraculous.

Then Wesley noticed there was a podium with a microphone in the center of the room. He went and talked into the microphone and spoke about Mr. Paul. I can't remember what he said, but my husband and I were laughing and crying at the same time. We left there feeling light. Now, Wesley was not asking where Mr. Paul was. In fact he has never asked again. He will say that Mr. Paul is in heaven, but his bones are in the cemetery.

We knew that Wesley needed concrete answers. We knew that he needed visual answers.

Several years later, Wesley lost his beloved grandfather to cancer. Once again, we were very open and honest with Wesley during the illness and eventual death. This time it was easier. Mr. Paul had helped us and shown us the way. We knew that Wesley needed concrete answers. He needed visual answers. He needed to go to the funeral home, he needed to see the casket, he needed to go to the cemetery, and he needed to know where his Gil was laid to rest.

So, where is Mr. Paul? I believe he is in heaven watching over Wesley. I still feel his presence and Wesley still speaks of him every now and then. He taught us much in life and kept teaching us in death.

Suzie Heaton, 2006

Message from the Author

Why did I write this book?

Most people do not like to think about death. Most people do not like to talk about death. But all people have to face the death of someone they know, sooner or later.

I wrote this book to make it easier for people to think and talk about death and dying, and about what they feel is most important in life. This book provides plain information, simply and clearly. I wrote this book to help people understand that death is part of life. Everyone's life. It allows the readers to review their experiences, and helps them express their thoughts and ask questions. It explains popular suggestions for living a good life.

Children and adults on the autism spectrum have taught me that it is is imperative to communicate most clearly about things that are the most difficult to understand. I first began writing this book specifically for young people with ASD and their families, although as I wrote, I discovered that there are others—including adults with ASD and neurotypical children and adults—who find it helpful.

It was during the last breaths of my father-in-law Paul Faherty, many years ago, that I learned how to sit in prayerful surrender. Paul's faith and gentle strength served as a compass guiding him through his physical pain. The memory of being with Paul during his sacred transition shepherded me through the deaths of people in my life occurring within a recent twelve-month period of time. From September 14, 2005 to September 14, 2006—to the day—I had to face deaths of several people close to me, and in doing so, I learned more about life.

My beloved father, Nicholas Collins, taught me how an old person can die naturally and peacefully—full of dignity, gratitude, and love after a long fulfilling life. My dad enjoyed his journey through life with curiosity, empathy, and generosity. I witnessed these same qualities carry him bravely into the greatest Unknown.

My friend and fellow TEACCH colleague, Sara Handlan, a master teacher in the prime of her talented and passionate life of service to families, children, and adults with ASD, showed me how a person is able to look ahead with eyes-wide-open honest courage. With true grace, Sara prepared herself and her family, friends, and clients for her own impending death coming way too soon.

Eric Schopler, the Founder of TEACCH and a professional role model, showed me how humility and kindness can thrive simultaneously with perseverance and genius; and that a person does indeed live on after death. In the 1960's, Eric's bold assertion that mothers did not cause their children's autism was a huge paradigm shift, unorthodox and revolutionary. His legacy—founding a program that is based on respect, support, and understanding for parents, children, and adults with autism—continues to touch millions of families worldwide.

And finally, my extended-family-daughter Meta Bowers-Racine brought together our community through the horrendous shock of her sudden and unexpected death. Somehow she led us one step at a time headlong through the unbelievable. We learned to accept responsibility with our deepest pain and wide-open hearts as we guided her from one life to the next—physically and spiritually.

Facing the deaths of people close to me this past year, propelled me on a personal and professional journey, resulting in this book.

My cousin Minas ("Mickey") Vassos died unexpectedly two weeks ago, while his sister Irene and I worked together during the final layout phase of this book. His last email message, written to both of us (unknowingly the day before he would die) expressed pride in our strong familial bonds, and his hope and belief that this book will be of great help to people. Minas exemplified the spirit of courage. He survived a wounded childhood, all along bringing light-hearted mischief and humor to his endeavors and relationships. In what was to be the last year and a half of his life, he courageously faced his past trauma with love and forgiveness. He told me many times during this year that his goal was to heal himself so he could become the best father he could be to his two children. It was courage that fueled Minas with the strength to keep on loving and to forgive. It was when Minas passed away that I realized that I needed to add the quality of **courage** to Chapter 16.

I dedicate Chapter 16 to my cousin Minas Vassos.

Why should you read this book?

Death and illness affect every person, young or old, male or female, neuro-typical or autistic. Witnessing and living through the dying and death of a person or pet can be a pivotal experience for those of us still here.

Death and illness affect every person, young or old, male or female, neurotypical or autistic. Witnessing and living through the dying and death of a person or pet can be a pivotal experience for those of us still here. Susan Moore, M.A. in her article, "Stages of Grief in Children," for the California Sudden Infant Death Syndrome Program, reports that "a child's fears and fantasies are usually far worse when they are not told what has happened in a clear and precise way."

In this book, I attempt to answer questions about illness, death, and dying in an autism-friendly, "clear and precise way." I have provided **Communication Forms** to make it easier for the readers and their families, friends, teachers, therapists, and others to identify and respond to the unique needs and concerns of the reader.

However, this book is not just about illness, death, and dying. It demonstrates the interconnectedness of living and dying by introducing concepts that come to the forefront when people face death. It encourages the reader to reflect on his or her own life and offers simple, positive guidelines for living.

Who should read this book?

Although I wrote it for people with ASD, it may be helpful for others—family members and friends as well.

The clear, concrete, and literal writing style is especially geared for children, teens, and adults with autism spectrum disorders (ASD) with solid reading comprehension skills. Although I wrote it for people with ASD, it may be helpful for others—family members and friends as well.

I encourage parents of younger children, and guardians of older family members with ASD who cannot read or comprehend the text; to read it on their own, and then explain, adapt, and/or illustrate the relevant information according to the unique needs of the individual family member, friend, student, or client. The following pages contain suggestions for how to do this.

Using This Book

When should it be read?

If a person or animal in the life of the reader is very ill and close to death, or has already died, **now** may be a good time to read this book. Perhaps a parent or guardian, family member, friend, teacher, or therapist will determine when to introduce selected topics. Some readers may look through the **Table of Contents** and choose their own topics of current concern. Even if someone's death is not imminent in the person's life, it may be educational for him or her to read selected chapters. Older or more sophisticated readers may choose to read the book from beginning to end, guided by their interest, need, and curiosity.

Is it about both people and animals?

Yes. There certainly are topics that are more pertinent for people. However, much of the information may be helpful when facing the deaths of beloved animals. The word "animal" or "pet" may often be substituted for the word "person."

How is this book organized?

The **Table of Contents** is organized by topic. **Communication Forms** generally follow each topic.

What are the "Communication Forms"?

The **Communication Forms** are multiple-choice lists to engage the reader and to support self-knowledge by inviting the reader to indicate what is true for him or her. The **Communication Forms** help the readers connect with others by promoting interaction with their communication partners about illness, dying, death … and significant aspects of life.

A Close Look at Communication

Many children and adults with ASD are quite verbal with adequate (or superior) vocabularies. At home and at work, neurotypical people assume that children and adults who can talk will ask questions or confide in them about their emotional, mental, and physical states of being—especially when needing help, wanting information, or correcting misunderstandings.

Effective communication can be challenging for everyone. However, it can feel like an unsolved mystery when it is between people with distinctly different styles of communication: neurotypical and autistic.

Neurotypical people and their communication partners with ASD are encouraged to think in terms of making new agreements about how to communicate.

People with ASD may make other assumptions, depending on the individual. Your child may assume that you know his or her thoughts and feelings. Your friend with ASD may choose not to communicate unless she or he can find the most precise and impeccably accurate wording. Your co-worker with ASD may unquestioningly assume that things are supposed to be the way they are—so there is no need to do or say anything that would result in a change.

Effective communication can be challenging for everyone. However, it can feel like an unsolved mystery when it is between people with distinctly different styles of communication.

In my years as a teacher and TEACCH therapist, working with both children and adults with ASD, I have learned that communication happens more easily when assumptions and behaviors are examined—and changed when necessary. I encourage neurotypical people and their communication partners with ASD to think in terms of **making new agreements** about how to communicate. Read on for suggested guidelines.

If you are a person with a mostly neurotypical (non-autistic) style of communicating, read Chapter 5 and consider adopting the six guidelines on the following page.

1. Wait. Don't expect a response to your questions or comments immediately.

Don't assume that you are being ignored if there is silence or refusal to answer. Allow time for the autistic communicator to process your questions and respond later. Doing otherwise sometimes forces a routine response from the person; "I don't know," or "Okay," or "No problem," just because he or she is expected to say something. By giving more processing time, you may become more patient ... and his or her responses may be more accurate.

2. Speak literally and concretely.

Avoid hinting and indirectness. "Beating around the bush" to be polite is not helpful. In fact the opposite is true, and unnecessary confusion may result. Say what you mean and mean what you say. No more, no less. By doing so, you will automatically communicate more honestly ... and your communication partner will more easily understand you.

3. Imagine.

Sit back and try to see through the eyes of the person with ASD. By doing so, you will more easily understand him or her.

4. Provide information.

Do not assume that the person knows what "everyone knows." Provide daily schedules, work systems, and structured visual communication support as taught by **TEACCH**. Write Social Stories™ to share accurate and relevant information, as taught by **The Gray Center for Social Understanding**. By doing so, you will help the person with ASD make sense of the world around him or her.

5. Provide communication tools.

Use paper, pen, computer, checklists, and other visually structured forms. Utilize a variety of visual methods such as list-making, semantic organizers, mind-maps, having a written conversation by sitting side by side at a computer, email, providing multiple-choice lists (as demonstrated on the **Communication Forms** in this book) and other individually designed visual supports. By doing so, you will make it easier for the person on the spectrum to communicate ... and you will strengthen your connection to him or her.

6. Realize that the autistic style of communicating is different from, but not inferior to, your more familiar neurotypical communication style.

By doing do, mutual appreciation and respect may flourish.

If you are a person who uses an autistic style of communicating (or if you are on the autism spectrum), read Chapter 5 and consider adopting these six guidelines:

1. Try to express yourself to the important people in your life.

Important people may include family members, friends, teachers, therapists, and others who care about you, and those whom you care about. Try to communicate even if it sometimes seems frivolous or unnecessary. Say that you need more time to think before responding, when needed. Use visual and/or written methods if helpful. By expressing yourself honestly, others may understand you better, and stronger connections may result.

2. Identify your needs, wants, hopes, questions, and fears.

Find words to describe them. By doing so, your self-knowledge will grow.

3. Ask for help when needed.

Say or write what isn't going well. Choose to believe that there often are ways to make things better. Get help thinking about possible solutions. By doing so, you will become truly responsible for yourself.

4. Say "thank you" or write "thank you notes" after someone has given you something.

Realize that you have been given something when someone has literally given you something material; done something for you; helped you make connections with someone or something; or has helped you in another way. By thanking people, you will become more responsible in relationships with others.

5. Know that others may have different ideas, opinions, understandings.

This is okay. Each person has his or her own thoughts and feelings, largely based on his or her individual life experience. Sometimes another person's perspective (their ideas, thoughts, feelings, etc.) will match yours. Sometimes they don't. This is natural.

6. Realize that the more common, neurotypical style of communicating is different from, but not inferior nor superior to, your natural autistic communication style.

By doing do, mutual appreciation and respect may flourish.

What is the purpose of Chapter 18?

Sophisticated readers may gain additional insight by reading what has been said by people who have thought about and written about aspects of life and death. Throughout the book you will encounter periodic notations referring to **Chapter 18**. These notations indicate that a related quote can be found in **Chapter 18**, easily located by its number in sequence.

How can this book be adapted for young children or adults who cannot read nor comprehend the text?

Parents, guardians, teachers, and therapists are invited to consider these seven suggestions:

1. Read the chapters that are relevant to the person you are assisting.

Try to see things literally, from his or her point of view. Your goal will be to provide this information visually, using actual photos of the real life situation.

2. Photograph locations, items, people, and events prior to, during, and/or after the death of the significant person or pet.

For example, take photos of the hospital, the funeral home, the hearse, the church, the cemetery—whatever pertains to the real life situation.

3. Get prepared prior to taking the photos.

First, highlight information in the relevant chapters of this book to remind yourself to get pictures of certain details. Make a list of these details. Keep your list and camera with you so you will always be ready to take the photos you need.

Keep in mind that young children or older individuals who have a young or very basic level of understanding will probably benefit more from the literal descriptions about what is actually happening around them, (the person in bed, the funeral, etc.) rather than the more abstract information in this book which introduces ideas and philosophies.

It is understandable that you may feel uncomfortable about pulling your camera out during such emotional and personal experiences. You may choose to explain to family members that you are taking pictures to help the involved child or adult understand what is happening. Or you may simply take photos quietly and respectfully, knowing that your intent is honorable. You can explain later.

4. Be open to spontaneous photos of significant items, people, or events.

For example, while visiting a person in the hospital, you may have planned to take photos of details in the room, the furniture, the places for visitors to sit, special equipment, and the person in bed. However, if a visiting family member happens to hold the hand of the person who is in bed, go ahead and take a photograph of this gentle, loving moment.

5. Tape the photographs on plain sheets of paper.

Write captions with the location, the date, and other concrete, relevant information. You can laminate the pages and keep them in a notebook. Reviewing the photos for days, weeks, months, and even years after the events may help the person process the information and make sense of the changes in his or her life.

6. Provide photographs for the child or adult even if he or she is able to read and comprehend this book.

Seeing actual photographs of the real-life situation may help him or her more easily digest, interpret, and retain the written information.

7. Use the type of illustration that is most meaningful for the individual.

Some children and adults may respond more easily to generic drawings or picture symbols like those offered on the Internet website: Do2Learn.com, or from software such as Boardmaker™. Hand-drawn pictures may be effective. Combinations of different types of pictures—all of the above—may be helpful to some children and adults.

8. If possible, use photos to prepare the person ahead of time, before taking him or her to the hospital, the cemetery, etc.

Use the photos afterwards, to help him or her review and process the experience.

What can I do for a child or an adult who does not read with comprehension, nor seem to understand pictures or photographs?

Keep in mind that the reason this book was written is to help people understand that death is a part of life. It is not to be feared. The transition of death can be embraced, with acceptance and peace. And life goes on.

For concrete thinkers and/or children and adults whose cognitive skills are significantly below average, or for those who—for any reason—are not helped by verbal explanations; the message is exactly the same: **Death is a part of life. It is natural. It is one of the transitions that occur in life. Sometimes important people and animals—parents, caregivers, teachers, pets, siblings, friends—leave and don't come back. They may go away or they may die. There is sadness and yearning. But there are things to look forward to—life does go on.**

Help the person literally see that life will go on, today and tomorrow. TEACCH Structured Teaching strategies give the person a familiar tool for engaging each day in a positive and proactive manner, despite big changes and puzzling transitions. Familiar structure offers predictability, and with it the comfort and assurance that life does go on. And isn't that the message?

TEACCH Structured Teaching strategies give the person a familiar tool for engaging each day in a positive and proactive manner, despite big changes and puzzling transitions. Familiar structure offers predictability, and with it the comfort and assurance that life does go on. And isn't that the message?

Children and adults who have mastered the use of schedules, checklists, work systems, communication systems, and other visual methods pioneered by TEACCH in the 1970s, have a solid foundation from which to handle transitions and change from the normal routine. They are resilient. They have learned to cope with small day-to-day changes—even last minute changes—by checking their daily schedules to see what to expect, moment by moment. Entries on the schedule may change, but the changes are made more understandable by being additions, deletions, or substitutions within the schedule as a whole.

They literally see that life goes on after these changes, and they see also that some things will stay the same. Most importantly, they have a way in which to predict what is actually going to happen—even if it is a change from their normal routine.

If the child or adult you are helping is unfamiliar with visually structured teaching strategies such as "the schedule," it is not too late to start. Show what is going to happen at each transition during the day by introducing visual cues that are most easily understood by the particular person: objects, pictures, or a written list.

Show the sequence of the day's activities on a pictorial or written list, or hand the person one picture or one object at a time, thus showing him or her "what is next." Even last-minute changes can be indicated in this manner. In this way you will provide reassurance that even though things change, there is a way to predict what is going to happen next.

Show the sequence of the day's activities on a pictorial or written list, or hand the person one picture or one object at a time, thus showing him or her "what is next." Even last-minute changes can be indicated in this manner. This is a way that you will provide reassurance that even though things change from day to day, hour to hour, there is a way to predict what is going to happen next.

Provide visual cues to encourage spontaneous communication, especially cues to make it easy to ask for help in stressful moments. Teach him or her to hand you a "help" card. The card may say "help" or it may show an entire written phrase to prompt speech. For others, it may be a photograph of the teacher or person who is available to help, or it may be a picture symbol representing "help." Use which works best for the individual.

Isaac doesn't talk much, and even if this book had been available when his grandmother died, he would not have been able to read it. He was fourteen and had a special bond with his beloved Grandmama. He had been to the hospital to see her as she lay dying. Afterwards, at the funeral home, his parents asked that the doors be closed so they would not be interrupted. Standing together at the casket, they lifted up Grandmama's arms, allowing Isaac to feel the cold lifelessness of her body, saying that she had died. Later at the grave, the casket was opened so he could see her body again, and say goodbye. Weeks later when they drove past the cemetery, Isaac softly said, "Grandmama."

Special Note to Parents and Significant Others

Write a letter containing thoughts or messages that you want to leave behind for your loved one.

Write a letter containing thoughts or messages that you want to leave behind for your loved one. You may choose to insert a photograph or two. Especially helpful for many individuals on the autism spectrum, written information allows for easier and greater comprehension of important topics. It is one way to pass on what you regard as important.

Update or revise the letter as time goes on. Make copies and place in a safety deposit box or another secure place where it will be found when you are gone. Give copies to dependable people to safe-keep and personally give to your loved one.

With today's digital technology, you may also choose to create an audio or video recording of talking, singing, or sharing in another way.

For both readers and non-readers, you may want to place a significant object or trinket that the person associates with you, along with your photos, in a special box for the one you leave behind.

You may want to place a significant object or trinket that the person associates with you, along with your photos, in a special box for the one you leave behind.

Thank you to my mother Ismene Collins for this idea.

Important Information For The Reader

What should I read first?

I may read this book in order from the beginning to the end. Or, I may look through the **Table of Contents** and choose the topics I am most interested in, and read those first.

What are the Communication Forms?

The **Communication Forms** are meant to help me think about how the information in the book applies to my life. Even though most of the time people do not write in books, the author of this book invites me to mark what is true for me with a pen, pencil, and/or highlighter pen. I may also write on the blank lines. I may write by myself, or I may dictate to someone else who will write it in for me.

After writing on the forms, I should show them to someone. The best person to show it to may be a parent or other family member, therapist, teacher, friend, or another trusted person.

The **Communication Forms** are also meant to help me communicate with other people. After marking each form, I should show it to someone. The best person to show it to may be a parent, other family member, therapist, teacher, friend, or another trusted person. It may be the person who gave me this book. The person I show the **Communication Forms** to may want to respond to what I have marked by talking or in writing to me.

The **Communication Forms** will help me learn more about myself. By showing the **Communication Forms** to other people, they may understand me better.

CHAPTER 1: Illness and Injury

Why do people get sick?

Illness is a normal part of life. Everyone gets sick at one time or another.

Illness usually is felt somewhere in or on the body. Some illness may not be felt.

Some illnesses are from viruses which may be passed from person to person through the air or through physical contact.

Some illnesses come from bacteria in the environment: from food, drink, objects, people, or animals.

Some illnesses result from genetic factors, meaning that they are a part of a person's make-up from birth.

There are many illnesses for which the causes are still unknown to science.

Different cultures and thinkers throughout time have tried to answer the question, **"Why do people get sick?"** Most of the current scientific research in the modern medical field is focused on trying to answer this question.

Communication Form

☑ I will check what is true for me.

☐ I have been sick.

☐ I am sick now.

☐ I know someone who is sick, now.

☐ I do not know the reason for the illness.

☐ I do know the reason for the illness. It is ______________________________

____

☐ I have questions or something to say: _________________________________

____

Is Asperger's an illness?

No. Asperger's and other autism spectrum differences are not illnesses.

Asperger's does not mean that a person is sick, or wrong. It is a person's natural way of being.

At the time of the writing of this book, current research reports that one person in every 150 people is on the autism spectrum (many of whom have Aspergers.)

Asperger's is considered to be on the autism spectrum. Sometimes the following terms are used:

- **Asperger's Syndrome (AS)**
- **autism**
- **high functioning autism (HFA)**
- **autism spectrum disorder (ASD)**
- **pervasive developmental disorder (PDD)**
- **pervasive developmental disorder not otherwise specified (PDDNOS)**
- **non-verbal learning disability (NLD)**
- **or another term:** ______________________________

Asperger's affects the way a person naturally experiences the world around him or her. Asperger's may help people have strengths, talents, or special skills. Asperger's also causes differences that may make certain aspects of everyday life challenging. Each person with Asperger's has his or her own strengths and challenges. It is not an illness.

All children and adults, including people with Asperger's, sometimes get sick and sometimes get hurt.

See Chapter 18 - Quote 1

Communication Form

☑ I will check what is true for me.

- ☐ I have never read or heard about Asperger's, or another term listed on the previous page.
- ☐ I will highlight or underline the term(s) that have been used with me.
- ☐ I want to know more about Asperger's, or another term that was listed. I will circle the term(s) which interest me.
- ☐ I do not want to know more about Asperger's, or another term that was listed.
- ☐ I have questions or something to say: ______________________________

  ____

How do I know if I am sick?

People typically experience symptoms when they are sick. "Symptoms" are sensations in the physical body that can be felt, seen, smelled, or otherwise detected. The sensation(s) may feel different than what or how a person usually feels.

Symptoms may vary, depending on the type of illness. Often, symptoms are the clues that help doctors figure out the name of the illness. Sometimes people experience different symptoms for similar illnesses, or similar symptoms for different illnesses. That is why it is helpful to get the help of a doctor or other health practitioner when trying to understand the relationship between symptoms and illness.

If a person is not sure if he or she is sick, it is a good idea to talk about it with a friend, family member, or another trusted person.

Common symptoms of different illnesses are included on the following list. Many symptoms are not on this list. (The list would be too long if the author had tried to list the symptoms of all illnesses!)

- Shaking or shivering
- Rash (redness) on skin
- Continual itching sensation
- Facial skin more pale than usual
- Facial skin more flushed than usual (pinkish or reddish)
- Body temperature more than 98.6 Fahrenheit.
- Soreness in or around eyes
- Soreness in other parts of body
- Wanting to sleep much more than usual
- More tired than usual
- Not being able to sleep when the person usually sleeps
- Tightness in throat when swallowing
- Blood (red tint) in urine
- Blood (red tint) in feces

- Redness or blood in throat or nose
- Sneezing or dripping from nose
- Difficulty or different sensation while breathing
- Different sensation in stomach area
- Diarrhea (loose or liquid feces)
- Vomiting ("throwing up") or gagging
- Other: ______________________________
- Other: ______________________________

Communication Form

☑ I will check what is true for me.

☐ When I experience a symptom on the list, or another symptom that I wonder about, I have someone with whom to talk about it.

☐ His or her name is ______________________________

☐ His or her phone number is ______________________________

☐ His or her email address is ______________________________

☐ I do not have anyone with whom to communicate when I am sick, or when I wonder if I am sick.

☐ I would like to have someone to communicate with when I think I may be sick or hurt.

☐ I know someone else who is sick, now. His or her name is __________

☐ I have questions or something to say: ______________________________

____

How do I know if I am injured?

Often people will sense a difference in the physical body when an injury occurs. However, some people may not sense an injury when it occurs.

An injury sometimes occurs as a result of an accident. Usually accidents happen suddenly and unexpectedly. Accidents include events such as falling down, dropping, breaking, or bumping into something. Accidents may involve equipment such as electrical items, tools, kitchen knives, furniture, bicycles, automobiles, or other items.

It is a good idea to check to see if an injury has resulted after an unexpected accident. Check the part of the body that was involved in the accident.

Sometimes an injury may not be sensed during or immediately after an accident. Some injuries become more apparent minutes, hours, or even days after the accident.

If a person is not sure whether he or she has been injured, it is a good idea to talk about it with a trusted person, such as a family member, friend, or someone else.

Common symptoms when injured are:

- Sensation of pain
- A strong sensation that may not have been there before
- Bleeding
- Swelling of a part of the body
- Redness of the skin
- Walking differently (limping, slower speed, etc.)
- Difficulty moving a part of the body
- Shaking or trembling
- A part of the body that looks or feels or moves differently than usual

Communication Form

☑ I will check what is true for me.

- ☐ When I experience a symptom on the list, or another symptom that I wonder about, I have someone with whom to communicate.
  - ☐ His or her name is______________________________
  - ☐ His or her phone number is ____________________________
  - ☐ His or her email address is____________________________
- ☐ I do not have anyone to tell when I may be injured.
- ☐ I would like to have someone to communicate with when I am injured.
- ☐ I know someone who is injured, now. His or her name is______________
- ☐ I have questions or something to say:__________________________

  ____

What should I do when I am sick or injured?

Sometimes illnesses and injuries cause the person to stay home from work, school, or other activities outside the home. This is okay.

Employers and teachers understand that people usually should not work when they are sick. Some injuries or illnesses may prevent a person from doing the work.

There are periods of time, or stages of some illnesses that may be contagious, which means that the sick person should have minimal physical contact with other people. However there are some illnesses or injuries may allow the person to continue with most of his or her daily activities as usual. It depends on the type, severity, and stage of the illness or injury.

It is customary, necessary, and/or thoughtful for a person to communicate with someone when they are sick or injured. Teachers, supervisors, friends, or other people will not know why the person is absent, unless they are notified.

A sick or injured person may call someone on the phone or send an email saying that he or she is sick or injured. If the person is supposed to be at work, it is necessary to notify the supervisor at work.

Sometimes a person may not be sure if he or she is sick or injured. In this case, it is a good idea to talk with a family member, friend, or other support person, to determine if something specific should be done.

Some people may not feel pain or other sensations when they are sick or injured. In these cases, it may be determined that even though the person does not feel pain, the injury or illness must be treated in order for healing to take place.

Communication Form

☑ I will check what is true for me.

☐ When I am sick or injured, I have someone with whom to communicate:

- ☐ His or her name is ______________________________
- ☐ His or her phone number is ______________________________
- ☐ His or her email address is ______________________________

☐ If I have a job, there is the person who needs to know when I am sick or injured:

- ☐ His or her name is ______________________________
- ☐ His or her phone number is ______________________________
- ☐ His or her email address is ______________________________

☐ I do not have anyone to email, call, or talk to when I am sick or injured.

☐ I would like to have someone to email, call, or talk to when I am concerned about being sick or injured.

☐ I have a doctor or other trusted medical professional. His or her name and contact information is ______________________________

____

☐ I have questions or something to say: ______________________________

____

What is an emergency?

An emergency is a sudden event that has caused (or may quickly cause) a very dangerous or life-threatening problem.

It is important to get help in an emergency. It is a good idea to have someone to call. Some emergencies require that a person immediately call 911.

Communication Form

☑ I will check what is true for me.

☐ I have never experienced an emergency.

☐ I have experienced an emergency in the past.

☐ I do not know who to call in an emergency.

☐ My emergency contacts (names and numbers) are the following:

- ☐ Name and contact info:____________________________________
- ☐ Name and contact info: ___________________________________

☐ Here is a list of specific types of emergencies which usually require calling 911. I should make this list with a trusted person.

____

____

____

____

☐ I would like more information about what to do in emergencies.

☐ I have questions or something to say about emergencies: _____________

____

What is a difficult situation?

A "difficult situation" may not be life-threatening, but may cause a person to become very worried, anxious, scared, and/or angry.

It is important to get help in a difficult situation. It is a good idea to have a person to call.

Communication Form

☑ I will check what is true for me.

☐ I have never experienced a difficult situation.

☐ I have experienced a difficult situation in the past.

☐ I do not know who to call in a difficult situation.

☐ My contacts (names and numbers) are:

- ☐ Name and contact info: ______________________
- ☐ Name and contact info: ______________________

☐ Here is a list of examples of difficult situations which would require calling a trusted person first, instead of 911. I should make this list with the help of a trusted person: ______________________

____

____

☐ I would like more information about what to do in a difficult situations.

☐ I have questions or something to say about emergencies, difficult situations, or contacts: ______________________

____

Why should I practice the plan when an emergency is not really happening?

During a difficult situation or an emergency, most people become anxious, stressed, angry, shocked, or confused. Or they may experience other reactions. It may become difficult to think about what to do. If an emergency or difficult situation occurs, it is important for the people to know what to do.

Emergencies or difficult situations are considered rare events—they do not happen often. Some people may never experience an emergency, but they still have to be prepared with a plan.

Most people will experience a difficult situation sometime in their lives. They should be prepared with a plan.

Most of the time, the plan involves communicating with someone else.

It is a good idea to practice calling or communicating with one's emergency contacts or contacts for difficult situations. It is a good idea to practice every few months.

If people have practiced following their plan, it is more likely that they will know what to do in the event of an actual emergency or difficult situation.

Communication Form

☑ I will check what is true for me.

- ☐ I have practiced communicating with my emergency contacts and my contacts for difficult situations.
- ☐ I have not practiced calling my contacts.
- ☐ I do not know who to call in an emergency or difficult situation.
- ☐ I do not know what to do if I have to contact someone in an emergency or difficult situation.
- ☐ I know what to do, but I have not practiced doing it.
- ☐ I would appreciate someone helping me with this subject of what to do in the case of emergencies or difficult situations. I will show this chapter to someone I trust. I will show it to (name) ______________________
- ☐ I would like my plan to be written down so I can read it.
- ☐ I have questions or something else to say: ______________________

____

CHAPTER 2: Recuperating and Healing

What helps people recuperate and heal?

When people are sick or injured, they usually recuperate and heal. The words "recuperate" and "heal" mean to get well; to get healthy again.

Parents, support people, doctors, and nurses usually know what should be done to help people recuperate and heal.

Sometimes there are choices about what should be done, depending on the illness or the injury. Advice may vary depending on the philosophy or education of the person giving the advice.

Specific things may help one person, but the same things may not help another person. Each person may need something different in order to heal.

Some examples of things that may help people recuperate and heal, depending on the illness, injury, and the individual, are:

- Getting more rest or more sleep
- Taking more baths or showers
- Taking special kinds of baths
- Eating certain foods
- Drinking more water
- Drinking certain liquids
- Not eating certain foods
- Not drinking certain liquids
- Taking medicine
- Taking certain vitamins and minerals
- Getting injections
- Wearing certain things
- Using certain equipment
- Getting certain kinds of exercise
- Doctor appointments
- Chiropractic adjustments

- Physical therapy
- Massage therapy
- Other therapies and appointments
- Going for a walk
- Being outside in fresh air
- Staying inside
- Listening to certain types of music
- Quiet activities
- Meditating
- Praying
- Visiting with people
- Keeping the same daily routine
- Specific changes in the daily routine
- Staying home—not going to school
- Staying home—not going to work
- Going to school with certain precautions
- Going to work with certain precautions
- Other: ______________________________

Communication Form

☑ I will check what is true for me.

☐ Someone I know is recuperating and healing by doing certain things. I will highlight or underline the things on the list that he or she is doing.

☐ I am healing and recuperating from being sick or injured. I can circle the things on the list that I am doing to recuperate and heal.

☐ I have something to say, or questions to ask: ______________________

____

What may being sick teach us?

Wise people have said that we can learn from being sick. In that way, illness is considered to be a teacher.

We can ask ourselves questions about being sick and about the nature of the illness. By asking questions, we may learn new things. Sometimes we may know the answers, and sometimes we may not know the answers. Sometimes we may make guesses about the possible answers.

If we do not know the answers to our questions about being sick, we can ask someone or we can find the answers by reading. We can ask parents, therapists, doctors, nurses, or someone else who is knowledgeable about the illness.

Sometimes, the people we ask may not know the answers. The answer may still be "unknown to science." Sometimes we may be able to make an "educated guess" as to the answer.

An educated guess means that people who are familiar with the illness, and with our behavior, may have a good idea about the answer.

Some questions are listed on the following **Communication Form.**

The last question, "What can I do to improve my health?" may be answered by looking at the previous answers and thinking about our own behavior. We may then come up with a plan to help us stay healthy.

Sometimes there are no clear answers to these questions. That is okay. They are still good questions to consider and try to answer.

Communication Form

☑ I will check what is true for me.

The name of the illness (if known) is: ______________________________

Was it caused by a virus?

☐ Yes

☐ No

☐ Unknown.

If Unknown, what may be an educated guess? ______________________

Was it caused by a certain food or drink?

☐ Yes

☐ No

☐ Unknown.

If Unknown, what may be an educated guess? ______________________

Was it caused by something that I did, or did not do?

☐ Yes

☐ No

☐ Unknown.

If Unknown, what may be an educated guess? ______________________

What can I do to improve my health? ______________________________

____

I have something to say or questions to ask: ______________________

____

What does being injured teach us?

Wise people have said that we can learn from being injured. In that way, getting hurt and being injured is considered to be a teacher.

We can ask ourselves questions about the injury and why it hurts. By asking questions, we may learn new things. Sometimes we may know the answers, and sometimes we may not know the answers. Sometimes we may make guesses about possible answers.

If we do not know the answers, we can ask someone who may be knowledgeable about the accident or the injury. People to ask may be parents, therapists, doctors, nurses, or someone else.

Some questions are listed in the following **Communication Form**.

The last question, "What can I do to stay safe from future injuries?" may be answered by looking at the previous answers and thinking about our own behavior. We may then come up with a plan to help prevent injuries in the future.

Sometimes, no matter how careful we are, we have an accident. Most people experience injuries or accidents sometime in their lives.

Sometimes we may not know the answers to the questions. That is okay. They are still good questions to consider and try to answer.

Communication Form

☑ I will check what is true for me.

If I am *(or was)* injured, write the part(s) of the body which were injured:

____

Was it caused by an accident?

☐ Yes

☐ No

☐ Unknown.

If Unknown, what may be an educated guess? ____________________

If it wasn't an accident, what caused the injury? ____________________

☐ Unknown.

If Unknown, what may be an educated guess? ____________________

Was it caused by something that I did or did not do?

☐ Yes

☐ No

☐ Unknown.

If Unknown, what may be an educated guess? ____________________

What can I do to stay safe from future injuries? ____________________

____

I have something to say or questions to ask: ____________________

____

Do people and animals usually recuperate and heal after being sick or injured?

Usually when people or animals get sick or injured, they will recuperate and heal. Getting sick or injured is a part of life and happens to everyone.

Sometimes we get better quickly, without having to do anything different from the usual routine. Sometimes we get better by doing something new or changing how we do things.

Sometimes we get better in a day or overnight. Sometimes getting better takes a longer time.

Illness and injury happen to all people. It is normal. Most of the time, people and animals heal and recuperate from illness and injury.

After recuperating, are people the same as they were before they were sick or injured?

Usually when people or animals get better after an illness or injury, they recover completely.

Recovering completely means that they are mostly the same as before. They look the same as they did before they were sick or injured. They can do the things that they used to do. They feel the same.

Sometimes a person or an animal gets better, yet some things have changed.

Some illnesses or injuries result in physical changes. There may be a change in how the body feels, or how it moves. A person may walk differently or talk differently. A person may need help doing some of the things he or she used to do without help. A person may look different than before. Or there may be other changes.

It is important to remember that even though there may be physical changes after a person has been sick or injured, he or she is still the same person.

Communication Form

☑ I will check what is true for me.

- ☐ I know someone who was sick or injured, and now he or she is different in some ways. I will circle the ways he or she is different:
  - ☐ Walks differently than before
  - ☐ Talks differently than before
  - ☐ Eats differently than before
  - ☐ Face looks different
  - ☐ Other part of body is different
  - ☐ Needs help with ____________
  - ☐ Other:____________________
- ☐ I would like more information about the differences that I see in (name):

  ____

- ☐ I am recovering from being sick or injured. Some things about me are different from before. I will circle which things are different about me:
  - ☐ Walk differently than before
  - ☐ Talk differently than before
  - ☐ Eat differently than before
  - ☐ Face looks different
  - ☐ Other part of body is different
  - ☐ Need help with ____________
  - ☐ Other:____________________
- ☐ I have questions or something to say:________________________

  ____

What else may we learn from being sick?

Wise people suggest that there are other things we may learn from being sick. These other things are "lessons of the spirit."

Lessons of the spirit include some of the things we may think about while we are sick or while we are recuperating.

Being sick usually causes people to slow down and take a break from their normal routine. They might have to stay home instead of going somewhere. They might need to get help from other people.

Slowing down from the normal routine allows us to take the time to think about life. It may give us time to review what we have learned about life, and decide what we want to understand better. It may give us time to ask questions (to ourselves or others) about important things.

Common "lessons of the spirit" may be found in Chapters 16 and 17.

Communication Form

☑ I will check what is true for me.

☐ I am thinking about my life. I am thinking about ____________________

____

☐ I don't know what I am thinking.

☐ I am not thinking about anything in particular.

☐ I am interested in some of the topics in Chapters 16 and 17, or other chapters in this book. I will circle the topics of my interest in the **Table of Contents.**

☐ I have something to say or questions to ask: ____________________

____

Does everyone recuperate and heal, all of the time?

Most of the time, people recuperate after being sick or injured. Everyone gets sick and injured at one time or another. However, there are times when people who are very sick or who have been injured severely may die as a result of the illness or injury. Chapter 3 gives more information about dying after illness or injury.

How does a person who is sick or injured know if he or she is going to recuperate, or if he or she is going to die because of the illness or injury?

Most of the time, people recuperate.

If a person wonders if he or she might die as a result of being sick or injured, it is a good idea to ask a parent, other family member, doctor, or nurse. They will answer this question.

Communication Form

☑ I will check what is true for me.

- ☐ I do not wonder about dying when I am sick or injured. I do not have questions about this.
- ☐ I have an important question. **"Am I going to heal and recuperate, or am I going to die because of being sick or injured at this time?"**
- ☐ I need more information about the illness or injury I have.
- ☐ I do not need more information.
- ☐ When I have questions, these are the people I can ask. Their names are:

____

Is the person or animal going to recuperate, or going to die from the illness or injury?

It is a good idea to talk with a family member, friend, or doctor when wondering about recuperating and about dying.

Sometimes when someone has been hurt or sick for a very, very long time, he or she might not recuperate fully.

Or if the person or animal has a severe injury, as in the case of some accidents, he or she may have difficulty recuperating and the dying process may begin. At these times, usually the doctors and nurses tell the family members that the person or animal may die soon. This means that the doctor is making an "educated guess." An educated guess means that the doctor knows about many illnesses and injuries, and he or she knows if this particular problem will probably cause death to occur.

Or the doctor may make an educated guess that the person will probably recuperate and heal from the particular illness or injury.

It is okay to ask the doctor or a family member if a specific person or animal is going to die because of the illness or injury.

Asking questions is a good way of finding out the answers. Sometimes people will know the answers, but sometimes they may not know the answers. It still is intelligent to ask.

Information about dying after being sick or injured can be found in the next chapter.

Communication Form

☑ I will check what is true for me.

☐ I know someone who is sick or injured. His or her name is ___________

____

☐ I wonder if this person is going to heal and recuperate, or if he or she is going to die from the illness or injury.

☐ I am wondering **"Is (name) ________ going to die from this illness or injury?"**

☐ I have something to say, or other questions to ask: __________________

____

____

CHAPTER 3: Death and Dying: Who, What, When, Where, and How

What is death and dying?

Living things are made up of cells that work together to keep the body of the person or animal, or the plant, alive and functioning.

"Death" is the word used to describe the moment that cells of a body or plant stop functioning. When someone dies, their body is not physically alive anymore.

"Dying" is the word used to describe the process prior to the final moment of death. The dying process can happen suddenly, or it can last a long time. Sometimes people say "pass away" or "pass on" instead of the word "die."

If death happens suddenly and unexpectedly, as in the case of some accidents, the dying process is short.

For most people or animals, the dying process takes longer. Sometimes people or animals who are sick or hurt don't get better, even after the doctors and nurses and family members try to help them get better with good food, medicine, and special care. It is then understood that the person or animal is dying.

For those who are not sick or injured, dying happens when they get very old.

Communication Form

☑ I will check what is true for me.

☐ I know someone who has died. His or her name is____________________

☐ I do not know someone who has died.

☐ I know someone who is dying. His or her name is ____________________

☐ I do not know someone who is dying.

☐ I have something to say, or questions to ask: ________________________

____

What is a lifespan?

All people and animals have a lifespan. "Lifespan" is the term used to describe the period of time that begins at the birth of the physical body and ends at the death of the physical body.

All living things, including people and animals, have a lifespan.

When do people and animals die?

No one knows how long his or her own lifespan will be. No one knows exactly when he or she will die. No one knows exactly how long someone else's lifespan will be.

Communication Form

☑ I will check what is true for me.

☐ If I know people or animals who have died, here are their names and their lifespans:

____

____

____

☐ I have something to say, or questions to ask: ____________________

____

What is life expectancy?

By observing and studying living things, scientists have determined the average lifespan for many living things. Scientists call it "life expectancy."

For example, the average life expectancy of a Golden Retriever dog who is loved and well-taken care of by its human family, is about ten to twelve years. This is just an average. Sometimes a dog will die before reaching that age, and sometimes after that age.

Scientists have determined the average life expectancy for human beings. The average life expectancy for humans varies depending on the country they live in and other factors.

According to statistics on Wikipedia, an internet encyclopedia, the average life expectancy for people in North America, and in parts of South America, Japan, Australia, and Europe is approximately 75 to 80 years.

In some parts of South America, the average life expectancy is between 60 and 70 years.

In some parts of Africa, the average life expectancy is between 50 and 60 years.

It is important to remember that all of these statistics are only averages.

In actuality, people can often live longer than expected, or they may live fewer years than expected. (According to Wikipedia, the oldest human lifespan that has been reported is 122 years.)

Each person and animal has his or her own lifespan, and it may be different from the average life expectancy.

No one knows exactly what his or her actual lifespan will be. No one knows exactly when someone will die. It is one of life's mysteries.

Communication Form

☑ I will check what is true for me.

☐ I knew a person, or an animal, who died. His or her name, and age at the time of death: ______________________________

____

☐ I was surprised that he or she had died. I didn't expect him or her to die.

☐ I was not surprised. I expected that he or she was going to die soon.

☐ Other people or animals in my life who have died, are: ______________

____

____

☐ I have something to say, or questions to ask: ______________

____

How do people or animals die?

Generally there are three different ways of dying.

1. Some people and animals die after a period of time of sickness or injury.

2. Some people and animals die suddenly and unexpectedly.

3. Some people and animals die after they have lived a long life and are old.

More information about these three ways of dying is given in this chapter.

What does it mean when someone dies after being sick or injured?

One way of dying is when a person or animal has been sick or injured.

An illness may be so severe that it causes the dying process to begin.

Or if a person was injured in an accident, the injury may be so severe that it causes the dying process to begin.

When people say that someone is dying, it is understood that the person or animal may die soon, possibly within the year.

Usually no one is sure exactly how soon the person will die. Doctors and nurses have been with many people and animals who have been sick or injured and then died, so they may be able to guess when the person might die. It might be in hours, days, weeks, or months. But they are just making an educated guess.

No one knows for sure until the person or animal actually dies. Sometimes doctors and family members are surprised if the person dies sooner than they had guessed. Other times the person takes a long time to die. Sometimes a person may be dying for many months or years.

Communication Form

☑ I will check what is true for me.

☐ I know a person or animal who is dying because of being sick. His or her name is ______________________________

☐ I know someone who is probably dying because he or she was in an accident. His or her name is ______________________________

☐ I know someone who is probably dying after he or she has lived a long life and is very old. His or her name is______________________________

☐ If a person or people in my life have already died, I will write their names, with the date and approximate time of death here: ______________

____

____

☐ If animals in my life have already died, I will write their names, with the date and approximate time of death here: ______________

____

____

☐ I have something to say or questions to ask: ______________

____

What does it mean when someone has died suddenly?

Sometimes a person or an animal has an accident that causes death to occur immediately or very soon afterwards. Examples are auto accidents, accidents while working or playing, or from being in a war or another dangerous situation.

Sometimes a person or an animal has a health problem that causes death to occur all of a sudden. This means that he or she had not been sick, and no one expected that he or she was going to die. Family members and friends did not expect death to happen to this person so soon. Or perhaps the person was sick, but the symptoms were absent or unnoticed. Sometimes there is no explanation for a sudden death. People may not know why it happened.

This is why people sometimes say that "it is a shock," that the person died. People are surprised. A sudden death is unexpected.

Communication Form

☑ I will check what is true for me.

☐ I know someone who died suddenly.

☐ We know how it happened. This is what happened: ____________________

____

☐ We do not know how it happened. It is still a mystery.

☐ I have something to say or questions to ask: ____________________

____

What does it mean when someone has died of old age?

Some people and animals live a long life. Eventually they become very old.

Sometimes very old people live most of their days sitting or lying down. It might be difficult for them to walk because their bodies are tired. (A very old person may get sick, or fall down and get hurt more easily than a younger person.) Old animals spend most of their days lying down, too.

Sometimes very old people think about their life and memories they have of childhood or other times with people. Sometimes they think about being close to death. They might talk about it. Or they might not talk about it.

Most family members and friends understand that the very old person is getting close to the end of his or her lifespan. Dying of old age is natural and expected.

Communication Form

☑ I will check what is true for me.

- ☐ I know someone who is very old.
- ☐ He or she sometimes talks about childhood memories.
- ☐ I would like to hear some of his or her memories.
- ☐ He or she has talked about dying.
- ☐ He or she has not talked about dying.
- ☐ I know an animal who is very old.
- ☐ I have something to say, or questions to ask: ______________________

____

Do all old people and old animals die?

All people and animals die at the end of their lifespan. No one knows the exact lifespan for any individual person or animal.

Many grandparents, older people, and old animals can continue to live a long time before they die.

Communication Form

☑ I will check what is true for me.

☐ My grandparent(s) or great-grandparent(s) are all still alive. Or there are other elderly people in my life who are still alive. Their names and ages are: ____________________

____

____

☐ One or more elderly people in my life has already died. Their names and dates of their deaths are: ____________________

____

____

☐ I know an old animal or animals. Their names and ages are:____________________

____

☐ One or more old animals in my life have already died. Their names and dates of their deaths are: ____________________

☐ I have something to say, or questions to ask: ____________________

____

Where do people die?

People may die in different locations. They may be at home or somewhere else.

In some countries, elderly people sometimes live in a special home because they need help taking care of themselves. They may die in this special home.

Sometimes people who have been dying for a while may be in a Hospice facility where people are taken care of to help them die peacefully. Hospice is the name of an organization that specializes in helping people die peacefully.

In the case of accidents, a person may die at the site of the accident, in an ambulance or in a hospital. Or a person may die somewhere else.

Communication Form

☑ I will check what is true for me.

☐ I know someone who has died. I wonder where he or she was at the moment of death.

☐ I know where he or she was at the moment of death. Location:

____

☐ I know someone who is dying. I wonder where he or she wants to be at the moment of death.

☐ I want more information about this topic.

☐ I want to talk with my parents or a trusted friend or support person about this topic.

☐ I have something to say, or questions to ask: ______________________________

____

Where do animals die?

Animals may die in different locations.

They may be inside, at home. They may be at the veterinarian's office. They may be outside.

In the case of an accident, the animal may die at the site of the accident, or nearby.

Some animals who are very sick or very injured may want to be alone. Some animals find a quiet place to lie down and die peacefully.

Some animals may want to be near other animals or people when they are dying.

Communication Form

☑ I will check what is true for me.

- ☐ I knew an animal who died.
- ☐ I know where he or she was at the moment of death. The location was:

  ____

- ☐ I know an animal who is dying. I wonder where he or she will be at the moment of death.
- ☐ I want more information about this topic. I want to talk with my parents or a trusted friend or support person about this topic.
- ☐ I have something to say, or questions to ask: ____________________

  ____

Chapter 4: When Someone Is Dying

Who takes care of people when they are dying?

Sometimes family members and close friends take care of their family member who is dying at home.

Sometimes nurses or helpers come to people's homes to help the family members take care of the dying person.

If people are dying in a hospital or a special home, they are usually taken care of by doctors, nurses, and other professional helpers. Family members may help, too.

In some countries, people who are dying may be in a hospital, and family members and friends must come to the hospital to take care of them.

Animals who are part of a family are usually taken care of by their people or by a veterinarian.

Communication Form

☑ I will check what is true for me.

☐ I know a person or animal who may be dying. His or her name is:

____

☐ He or she is being taken care of by ________________________

☐ I want more information about this topic.

☐ I have something to say or questions to ask: ____________________

____

What happens to the body of the person or animal in the dying process?

When the body is dying, the person or animal is still alive. However, the body may be in the process of "shutting down."

Cells make up all the organs of the physical body. Organs are the heart, liver, stomach, pancreas, kidneys, lungs, skin, etc. The organs work together to keep us alive. When the body is dying, it usually means that the circulation of blood within the body becomes limited and less oxygen gets to the body's cells. When this happens, the cells slowly stop functioning and begin to die. This causes the organs of the body to begin to stop working, or to shut down.

When doctors or family members understand that the body is shutting down and probably will not recuperate, they say that the person or animal is dying.

During the dying process, the person or animal may look, act, or sound different than before.

Communication Form

☑ I will check what is true for me.

- ☐ I know a person or animal who may be dying. If I checked this statement, then I will check other statements below that are true about him (her).
    - ☐ He or she looks different than usual.
    - ☐ He or she acts different than usual.
    - ☐ He or she sounds different than usual.
    - ☐ Something else seems different about the person. ________________

      ____
- ☐ I have something to say, or questions to ask about the person or animal who may be dying: __________________________

  ____

Why do people visit a person who may be dying?

Sometimes people visit a person who is dying, especially if the person is a family member or close friend.

For example, grandparents who are dying may want to see their children or their grandchildren, so they hope the children will visit. Children and grandchildren may want to spend time with their parent or grandparent before he or she dies. Usually the person's husband or wife, children, brothers, sisters, cousins, and friends may want to visit the person.

Sometimes family members come from far away so they can visit the person who may die soon. It may be the last time that people may see the person while he or she is alive.

Communication Form

☑ I will check what is true for me.

☐ I know a person who may be dying. His or her name is ______________

☐ I have visited this person.

☐ I have not visited this person.

☐ I want to visit the person.

☐ I am not sure if I want to visit.

☐ I already have visited, and I want to visit the person again.

☐ I do not want to visit this person.

☐ Other people have visited this person.

☐ I have something to say or questions to ask: ______________________

____

What if a person feels uncomfortable about visiting someone who is dying?

Sometimes people may feel uncomfortable about visiting a person who is dying.

One reason this book was written it to help people get answers to their questions about death and dying. When people have more information about dying and death, and know what to expect, it may be more comfortable to visit someone who is dying.

Dying and death are **natural parts of life.** Everyone knows or will know people or animals who have died.

Communication Form

☑ I will check what is true for me.

- ☐ I am uncomfortable about visiting (name) ________ , who may be dying.
- ☐ I want to feel more comfortable about visiting (name) _______________ .
- ☐ I want more information about death and dying.
- ☐ What does it mean that death and dying are **natural parts of life?**
- ☐ I have something to say or questions to ask: _________________________

____

What may happen during a visit to a person who is dying?

The person's eyes may be closed or they may be open.

The person probably can hear what is being said, even if he or she seems to be sleeping.

The person may want to talk. Sometimes the person who is dying does not want to talk, or cannot talk.

The person may smile. The person may have tears in his or her eyes. The person may cry. The person may make other sounds, too.

The person may make a sound with each breath.

The visitors may touch the person softly or hold hands with the person.

The visitors may give the person a kiss.

It is okay to talk to the person even if their eyes are closed. It is also okay for visitors to ask questions.

Sometimes if the person is able to talk, he or she may have something to tell their family members and friends.

Visitors may talk with one another, too.

A nurse or another person may tell the visitors when the time for visiting is finished. Or the visitors may stay as long as they want.

Communication Form

☑ I will check what is true for me.

☐ I know a person who may be dying. His or her name is ______________

☐ I have visited this person.

☐ I have not visited this person.

☐ I want to visit this person.

☐ This person's eyes were closed the whole time during my visit.

☐ This person's eyes were open sometimes during my visit.

☐ This person spoke during my visit.

☐ I will underline or highlight the sentences on the previous page that describe my visit to the person.

☐ I have something to say or questions to ask: ______________________

____

What might it be like if the person is in a hospital?

People who are being taken care of in hospitals are called **patients**.

A patient may share a room with one other patient. Or there may be many patients sharing the same room. Often there is a curtain between the patients who are sharing a room.

Noises may be heard, like the noise of patients talking or moaning or breathing or watching TV. Or the patients may be quiet. Sometimes other patients will have visitors, too. The sounds of visitors talking may be heard.

Nurses and doctors walk in and out of the room, doing their jobs. Usually they will talk to the patient or the visitors. The patient or the visitors may ask the nurses or doctors for information or for help.

The patient may have tubes taped on his or her arms, face, or another part of the body. There might be a clear plastic bag hanging up nearby. If the tubes go from the bag to the person, this is probably the way the person is getting fluids, nutrition, or medicine.

If there are tubes going into the person's nose, then he or she is probably getting extra oxygen to help him or her breathe more easily. In some cases, there may be a machine that is helping the person breathe.

There may be other machines or equipment being used. Or there may not be any machines or equipment being used.

If equipment or machines are functioning, people may hear soft noises or periodic beeping sounds.

Communication Form

☑ I will check what is true for me.

- ☐ I know a person who is a patient in a hospital.
- ☐ I have visited this person.
- ☐ I have not visited this person.
- ☐ I want to visit this person.
- ☐ The person was (is) the only patient in the room.
- ☐ He or she is not the only patient in the room. There were a total of _____ patients in the room.
- ☐ Some sounds I heard and things I saw in the hospital were: ___________

  ____

  ____

  ____
- ☐ I will underline or highlight the sentences on the previous page that describe my hospital visit.
- ☐ I have questions about what I saw or heard in the hospital.
- ☐ I have something to say or questions to ask: ______________________

  ____

What if the person who is dying tries to talk?

Some people who are dying want to talk.

The person's voice may be weak and sound different than usual. He or she may whisper. Visitors should try to listen quietly and patiently to what the person is saying.

Sometimes people who are dying want to tell their family and friends that they love them. Sometimes they may ask questions. They may ask for help.

Some people who are dying may give advice to their family members and friends. They may make suggestions about how to live and what is important in life.

It is good to listen when the person is talking. It is okay to ask questions.

If it is true, it is wise and good to say "**I love you**" or "**I will miss you**" to the person who may die soon.

It is also okay to be quiet.

Some people may choose to write a note or letter to the person who may die soon.

Communication Form

☑ I will check what is true for me.

- ☐ When I visited, the person spoke, or tried to speak.
- ☐ I understood what the person said.
- ☐ This is what the person said:____________________________________

  ____
- ☐ I didn't understand what the person said.
- ☐ I want to ask another visitor to help me understand what the person said. I want to ask (name)________________to help me understand what the person said.
- ☐ I want to tell the person that I love him (her).
- ☐ I want someone else to tell the person for me, that I love him (her).
- ☐ I want to tell the person that I will miss him (her).
- ☐ I want someone else to tell the person for me, that I will miss him (her).
- ☐ I want to write a note or letter to the person, for him or her to read, or for someone else to read it to him (her).
- ☐ I want to write a note or letter to the person, and then I will read it to him (her).
- ☐ I want to visit the person and just sit quietly.
- ☐ I have something to say or questions to ask:__________________________

  ____

What if the person who is dying cannot talk?

The visitors can talk to the person who is dying, even if the person cannot answer. The person may not be able to talk, or the person may be asleep. Most doctors and nurses agree that even if the person appears to be asleep, he or she may still hear what people are saying.

Even if the person cannot talk, sometimes he or she may indicate that he has heard what was said by blinking eyes or moving in another way.

Visitors can tell the person about their school or work, what they are thinking about, and how they are feeling.

If it is true, it is good to say "**I love you**" or "**I will miss you**" to the person who is going to die soon.

It is okay to ask questions even if the person cannot answer. Maybe someone else will be able to answer the questions.

It is okay to write a note or letter to the person and then read it aloud to the person, or have someone else read it to the person.

Sometimes when a person sleeps for long periods of time, it is called "being in a coma."

The visitors may also talk to each other, or they may be quiet. Some visitors may be quiet, look at the person who is dying, and make eye contact with him or her.

It is okay to visit by sitting quietly with the person who is dying.

See Chapter 18 - Quote 2

Communication Form

☑ I will check what is true for me.

- ☐ I have visited a person who may be dying.
- ☐ The person cannot talk.
- ☐ The person communicated in other ways.
- ☐ The person did not communicate.
- ☐ The person appeared to be sleeping.
- ☐ I want to tell the person that I love him or her.
- ☐ I want someone else to tell the person for me, that I love him or her.
- ☐ I want to tell the person that I will miss him or her.
- ☐ I want someone else to tell the person for me, that I will miss or her.
- ☐ I want to write a note or letter, to be read to the person.
- ☐ I want to visit the person to sit quietly without talking.
- ☐ I have something to say or questions to ask: ________________________

____

What if the person who is dying does not want any visitors?

Sometimes the person who is dying does not want to see other people. A person who is close to death may want to be alone. It is natural for a person who is dying to want to be alone.

People who are dying may want to think their own thoughts and feel their own feelings, without interruption.

Or they may feel too sick or too uncomfortable to have visitors. They may not have enough energy to be with visitors.

If someone wants to communicate with a person who is dying, he or she can write a note or a letter and have it delivered.

Communication Form

☑ I will check what is true for me.

☐ I know a person who likes to have visitors.

☐ I know a person who does not want visitors, lately.

☐ I want the person to know that I love him (her).

☐ I want the person to know that I will miss him (her).

☐ I want the person to know that I will remember him (her).

☐ I will write a note or a letter to the person.

☐ I do not want to write a note or a letter to the person.

☐ I want someone else to write a note or letter for me. I would like (name)____________________ to write it for me. I will say what to write.

☐ I have something to say or questions to ask: ________________________

____

How do people react when someone they know is dying?

People have different reactions when they know someone is dying. A common reaction is that people feel emotions.

Some people feel sad. The sadness may feel soft and small, or it may feel big and deep. They may feel sad because they will miss the person being in their lives. Or they may be sad for other reasons.

Some people feel angry when someone is dying. There may be just a little bit of anger, or it may be a lot of anger. They may feel angry because the person is dying and won't be in their lives anymore. Or they might be angry for other reasons.

Sometimes people feel other emotions. Sometimes people feel two or more different emotions at the same time.

Sometimes people feel one emotion, and then they feel another emotion.

Sometimes people do not know how they feel.

Some people may not feel anything.

Some people are confused.

Most people have questions when someone is dying, or has died. The way to find out the answers to questions is by asking. It is a good idea to ask questions about death, dying, and living.

Chapter 13 is about people's reactions when someone dies.

Communication Form

☑ I will check what is true for me.

- ☐ Someone I know is probably dying. His or her name is ______________
- ☐ I do not know how I feel about the person dying.
- ☐ I feel emotions when I think of the person dying.
- ☐ I will check what is true for me. I may check one or more of the following. Sometimes I feel …
  - ☐ Sad about the person dying.
  - ☐ Okay about the person dying.
  - ☐ Angry about the person dying.
  - ☐ Frustrated about the person dying.
  - ☐ Afraid about the person dying.
  - ☐ Worried about the person dying.
  - ☐ Confused about the person dying.
  - ☐ Something else: ______________________________
- ☐ I want to read more about what happens when someone dies. I will look in the Table of Contents of this book for the questions I want answered.
- ☐ I have something to say or questions to ask: ______________________

  ____

What does it mean when people say it is time to "let him (her) go"?

Dying is compared to going on a journey.

The people who are still alive may find out that the time has come to say goodbye to the person or animal who is dying. The time has come to begin to **"let him go"** or **"let her go."**

Saying goodbye and letting the person or animal go helps him or her die peacefully. Dying peacefully is a good way to die. Friends and family members can help the person or animal die peacefully by **"letting him (her) go."**

People may think about the good times they had together. They may thank the person or animal for being in their lives. They may think or say or write down other things about the person who is dying.

Sometimes the person can die more easily and peacefully when he or she is alone, after the visitors leave the room. Sometimes the person wants a loved one to stay in the room.

"Letting go" is a wise and good thing to do when a person or an animal is dying.

It is okay to say goodbye, even though no one knows exactly when the person will die. No one knows exactly when death will come. The person may die soon after the "goodbye," or the person may live longer.

Communication Form

☑ I will check what is true for me.

- ☐ A person or animal I know is dying. I wonder if it is time to "**let him (her) go.**" I will ask a trusted person if it is time to begin to say goodbye.
- ☐ It is probably time for me to say goodbye and begin to let him(her) go.
- ☐ I am ready to let (name)______________________________ go.
- ☐ I am not ready to let (name)______________________________ go.
- ☐ I can ask someone to help me get ready to let the person (or animal) go.
- ☐ I want to visit the person (or animal) who is dying.
- ☐ I want to thank him or her for being in my life.
- ☐ I want to say goodbye.
- ☐ I want to tell him or her something else. I want to communicate this:

  ____

  ____
- ☐ There is something else I want to do before the person (or animal) dies. It is: ____________________________________

  ____

  ____
- ☐ I have questions or something to say: __________________________

  ____

CHAPTER 5: Communication

What is communication?

Communication is an action that allows one person (or group of people) to know and understand what another person (or group of people) is thinking or feeling. Communication is how people share ideas from one mind to another mind.

The act of communication is most frequently accomplished through talking or writing.

There are many other ways to communicate—through art, music, dance, and other art forms.

Another person (or group of people) receives the communication by hearing or reading or seeing or sensing what is being communicated.

In order for communication to be successful, the person **receiving** the communication must understand what is being communicated.

Communication Form

☑ I will check what is true for me.

☐ I will circle the ways in which I sometimes communicate:

- Talking face-to-face with another person
- Talking by phone
- Writing and sending emails
- Writing and mailing letters by post
- Manual sign language
- Using pictures or picture symbols
- Drawing or painting
- Computer graphics
- Singing
- Playing a musical instrument
- Dance or creative movement
- Writing stories or essays
- Writing poetry
- Other art form: ______________________________
- Talking about or showing someone things that I like
- Other: ______________________________
- Other: ______________________________
- It is usually easiest for me to communicate by the following method(s):

____

____

☐ I have something to say or questions to ask: ______________________________

____

Why is communication important?

Communication is often the first step in understanding one another. It is a direct way for people to connect with one another.

No one really knows what thoughts are in someone else's mind, or what feelings are in someone else's heart, unless the thoughts, ideas, or feelings are communicated.

Communication is considered by many people to be one of the most important activities in which a person can participate because it is a way to build connections with others.

Communication can help us understand one another. It can contribute to a more peaceful life.

Communication Form

☑ I will check what is true for me.

- ☐ There is something that people should understand about me. They should understand that ______________________

  ____

- ☐ I want to understand more about something or someone. I would like to understand more about ______________________

  ____

- ☐ I have something to say or questions to ask: ______________________

  ____

What does it mean to communicate "before it is too late"?

Sometimes people who are dying realize that they have something to communicate.

There might be something they want to tell a particular person. They hope they have time to communicate with the particular person before dying.

A family member or a friend may want to communicate with the dying person before he or she dies.

We do not really know when another person's lifespan will come to an end. We do not really know when our own lifespan will come to an end.

Facing someone's death reminds us that it is important to communicate with our family members, friends, and other people close to us while we are still alive.

Communication Form

☑ I will check what is true for me.

☐ There is something that I need to communicate. It is: ____________________

____

☐ There is a particular person with whom I need to communicate. His or her name is: ____ .

☐ I don't have anything that needs to be communicated at this time.

☐ I have something else to say or questions to ask: ____________________

____

What are some examples of the things that people may want to communicate before someone dies?

Examples of simple but important things that may be communicated are listed on this **Communication Form.**

No one really knows a person's thoughts or feelings for sure, unless they are communicated. It is wise to use this **Communication Form** by checking, writing, and showing it to a family member, friend, or other trusted person.

Communication Form

☑ I will check what is true for me.

☐ No one knows for sure when someone will die; however, it is believed that someone in my life may die soon, possibly within the next several days, weeks, months or year. If this is true, I will mark the statements on this **Communication Form** that are true for me.

☐ No one knows for sure when someone will die, so there are important things I want to communicate to someone in my life, even if he or she is not dying soon. I will mark the following statements that are true for me.

☐ I want (name)__________ to know something in particular that I am thinking or feeling, or something else about me. I want the person to know this:

____

____

☐ There is something to say or ask the person (name)____________ who is dying. It is this:

____

____

- ☐ I would like someone else to talk to (name) ________________ for me.
- ☐ I will mark the following things to communicate to (name)__________ .
- ☐ "Thank you for ____ ."
- ☐ "Thank you for being in my life."
- ☐ "I forgive you for ______________________________________ ."

(Information on forgiveness can be found in Chapter 16.)

- ☐ "I am sorry about______________________________________ ."
- ☐ "Please forgive me for something that I have done. What I did was _____ ____ ."
- ☐ "I will miss you."
- ☐ "I love you."
- ☐ I have something else to say or to ask. It is: ______________________ ____
- ☐ There is something to say, but instead of saying it aloud, I will write it down and give it to the person. I need paper and pen, or a computer to write it.
- ☐ I have nothing to say or ask right now. I might have something to say or ask, later.
- ☐ I have questions or something to say:___________________________ ____

How do people communicate effectively?

When people communicate effectively, they talk to another person at a time when the other person is able to pay attention and listen carefully. Or they write it and make sure that the other person receives the letter or message.

It is often necessary to make sure that the other person understands what is being said (or what was written). The speaker (or writer) may ask, "**Do you understand what I said?**" or "**Do you understand what I have written?**" If the person does not understand, then more information can be said or written.

Another part of communication is listening and trying to understand what someone else is saying. If the communication is written, the other person must be able to read and comprehend what has been written.

What is a miscommunication?

When a person tries to communicate, but other people are confused about what was said or written, it can be considered a **miscommunication.**

If what is being communicated doesn't make sense to the listener or the reader, it can be considered a **miscommunication.**

What should be done in cases of miscommunication?

After noticing that there may be a miscommunication, the listener may politely request that the speaker "**please explain it again.**" This is an intelligent and responsible thing to do when something is confusing or doesn't make sense.

Another option is for the listener to politely request that the speaker "**please write it down to make sure I understand.**" Asking for more explanation in written form is an intelligent and responsible thing to do.

Sometimes other people may say that they don't understand what I am saying. This may also be an example of miscommunication. If someone asks me to explain it again, it means that the listener or reader needs more information in order to better understand what I am saying.

It is intelligent and responsible to try to ask for—and to give—more information by talking or writing.

Communication Form

☑ I will check what is true for me.

- ☐ I prefer to communicate by talking.
- ☐ I prefer to communicate by writing.
- ☐ I would like to have a choice when communicating, sometimes talking, sometimes writing, sometimes listening, and sometimes reading.
- ☐ There are times when I do not understand what is being communicated.
- ☐ Sometimes I would like to **read** what a person is saying to me.
- ☐ When I don't understand, I usually am quiet. I usually don't say anything.
- ☐ When I don't understand, I usually ask the person to explain.
- ☐ I usually understand these people best:____________________
- ☐ I have trouble understanding these people:____________________
- ☐ I think that these people understand me best: ____________________
- ☐ These people usually don't understand me:____________________
- ☐ I have something to say or questions to ask:____________________

  ____

Why is understanding each other so important?

"Misunderstanding" means **not** understanding.

"Miscommunication" means that there is a problem with a specific attempt at communication.

Misunderstanding and miscommunication between people can be compared to there being thick walls between people. Thick walls between people would make it difficult for people to see, hear and, therefore, understand each other.

Understanding can be compared to the thick walls coming down between people.

When the "walls" are down, people are able to "see" each other more clearly. They are able to listen to each other. They may begin to understand each other better.

They may find out that even though people are different from one another, there are some ways that people are the same. Sometimes they discover that they have ideas, thoughts, dreams, desires, fears, feelings, or other experiences in common.

They may also learn to accept that there are differences between people. They may learn to respect other human beings, even though there are differences.

When people understand and/or respect each other, individual lives and society in general may improve.

One pathway to greater understanding is communication.

Communication Form

☑ I will check what is true for me.

- ☐ I think there is a misunderstanding or a miscommunication between me and someone else.
- ☐ There often are misunderstandings or miscommunications between me and someone else.
- ☐ The person or people I have misunderstandings or miscommunications with are: ______________________________

  ____
- ☐ I am not sure what is meant by "misunderstanding."
- ☐ I am not sure what is meant by "miscommunication."
- ☐ I have questions or something to say: ______________________________

  ____

"Understanding" Goes Two Ways:

Trying to understand someone else is a necessary part of communication.

There are a lot of people in the world, and there are many different beliefs and opinions.

Even when there is a disagreement, it is important to try to understand one another.

It takes strength of character to try to understand someone who has a different opinion.

Communication Form

☑ I will check what is true for me.

☐ There is something that I want to understand. It is: ____________________

____

☐ There is someone whom I want to understand better. The person is (name)____

☐ I want other people to understand something about me. It is: __________

____

☐ I have questions or something to say: ______________________________

____

How does someone know that he or she has something important to communicate?

There are at least three categories of communication for expressing oneself:

1. One category is communication that expresses the need for a change to make things better.

2. The second category is communication that expresses pleasure and gratitude about how things are.

3. The third category is communication that shares information about ideas, thoughts, or feelings.

Communication Form

☑ I will check what is true for me.

- ☐ There are times when I wish certain things would change for the **better**.
- ☐ There are times when I like to share information about some of my **ideas**.
- ☐ There are time when I like to share information about some of my **thoughts**.
- ☐ There are times when I like to share information about some of my **feelings**.
- ☐ There are times when I am **glad** that certain things are the way they are.
- ☐ Something else I want to say: ______________________________

  ____

The First Category: How does someone know that he or she should communicate to express the need for a change?

When a person feels discomfort, it is a clue that there may be a need for communication.

A person may notice that he or she feels emotions such as impatience, frustration, anger, sadness, anxiety, fear, confusion, or another uncomfortable feeling.

Physical sensations are sometimes clues to emotions that signal the need for communication. Some physical sensations are feeling a fluttering or heavy feeling in the stomach, a stomach ache, heaviness in the area of the heart, the heart beating rapidly or hard, tightness in the throat, itching skin, blushing, or another physical sensation.

Each individual has his or her own physical reactions to discomfort, confusion, and emotions.

When a person notices physical reactions in the body, it is the time to ask oneself, **"Is something bothering me?"** If so, then ask **"What is bothering me?"** Another important question to ask oneself is **"What do I wish was different about this situation?"**

Asking these questions to oneself—and answering them honestly—is a way to decide whether to communicate, and what specifically needs to be communicated.

Communication Form

☑ I will check what is true for me.

☐ Something is bothering me. It is: ____________________________

____

☐ I wish something would be different. It is: ____________________

____

☐ I have something to communicate. It is:______________________

____

☐ I don't know if something is bothering me.

☐ I will highlight or underline the words on the previous page that describe physical sensations that I sometimes experience.

☐ I experience another kind of physical sensation. It is ______________

☐ I sometimes experience those physical sensations when I am in these situations or locations:_______________________________

____

☐ I sometimes experience a physical sensation when I am near the following people: (names) _________________________________

____

☐ I have questions or something to say about this:_________________

____

What is "help"?

"Help" means "assistance doing or understanding something."

Asking for help is one important part of communicating.

One person may need help. Another person may be the helper. One person may need help sometimes, but be a helper at other times.

Everyone needs help sometimes. Everyone can help someone else, sometimes.

Here is a list of the different ways that a person may recieve help:

1. **The helper does it all.** The person asking for help watches or listens while the helper does it all.

2. **The helper tells the person exactly what to do.** Then the person does it.

3. **The helper does some of it, but not all of it.** This may happen in three ways:

- The helper may start it ... and the person asking for help may finish it.
- The helper waits for the person to get started ... and then the helper finishes.
- The helper and the person needing help work together.

4. **The helper may give suggestions about what to do.** The person needing help can choose what to do from the suggestions.

5. **The helper may ask questions that allow the person to think about it on his own.** Then the person figures out what to do, and does it by him- or herself.

6. **Other ideas of ways to help:**____________________________________

____

Communication Form

☑ I will check what is true for me.

☐ I would like help with something in my life. It is ____________________

____

☐ I do not need help with everything, but there may be one thing with which I need help currently. It is ________________________________

☐ I want help but do not know…

- ☐ WHEN to ask for help.
- ☐ HOW to ask for help.
- ☐ WHO to ask for help.

☐ The name or names of people whom I may ask for help are:___________

____

☐ I want (or need) help with this: ________________________________

____

☐ I do not want (or need) help.

(Information on indepenence and interdependence is in Chapter 16.)

☐ I have something to say or questions to ask: ________________________

____

The Second Category: How does someone know when he or she should communicate pleasure and gratitude?

People sometimes describe experiences or reactions that are called "positive." Positive experiences cause feelings of pleasure, joy, and happiness.

Positive experiences may cause people to react with a feeling of relief, satisfaction, comfort, contentment, peace of mind, or relaxation.

Positive reactions and feelings often happen automatically when something is going well in a person's life.

Or, a person may **choose** to experience life with a positive feeling, even when things happen that he or she doesn't like.

When a person learns to experience life with a feeling of gratitude and acceptance, positive feelings may be felt, even when things go wrong.

Information about keeping a positive attitude can be found in Chapter 16.

Communication Form

☑ I will check what is true for me.

☐ I sometimes have positive experiences. Some positive experiences I have had are: ______________________________

____

☐ I will underline or highlight the positive words on the previous page that are sometimes true for me.

☐ I want more information about positive reactions and positive feelings.

☐ I have questions or something to say: ______________________________

____

Why is it important to communicate gratitude when having positive feelings and experiences?

People often "take things for granted." This means that they may not notice some of the good things in life.

Sometimes people pay attention only to the things that they do not like. They may think too much about the people who bother them. They may complain too much about the things they do not like.

They may spend their time thinking about what they do not like about their lives. They may spend time thinking about what they lack, or what is missing from their lives.

If they spend time thinking only about what they do not like, then their days and nights will be filled with thoughts about things they do not like. It will feel as though their lives are full of things they do not like.

Wise people know that paying attention to what is good, being grateful for the good things, and communicating about the good things is one way to live a good life. They will feel that their lives are full of positive experiences.

Saying "thank you" is a powerful communication. It creates positive feelings and good connections with others.

Saying "thank you" to others and writing a list of "Good Things In My Life" are wise things to do.

Paying attention to what a person likes in his or her life and saying "thank you" may increase the chances of positive experiences continuing.

Information about "keeping a positive attitude" can be found in Chapter 16.

Communication Form

☑ I will check what is true for me.

☐ I mostly pay attention to the things that bother me and what I do not like in my life.

☐ I mostly pay attention to the things I like in my life.

☐ I usually notice both—the things I like and the things I do not like.

☐ I want to notice more positive things in my life. Some of the positive things are: ____________________

____

____

____

☐ The people I want to thank are (names) ____________________

____

____

____

☐ I have something to say or questions to ask: ____________________

____

Whom should I thank?

Saying "thank you" to others is a positive action.

There are people in my life who have helped me when I needed help. Some people have been in my life for a long time. Some people have helped me make connections with new people. Some people are happy for me when things are going well, and encourage me when I need support.

Communication Form

☑ I will check what is true for me.

☐ People who helped me when I was younger were ____________________

____

☐ People who help me now that I am older, are ____________________

____

☐ People who have encouraged me are ____________________

____

☐ People whom I can rely on are ____________________

____

☐ There is a person, or people, whom I may not have thanked yet. I want to say thank you to this person, or these people: ____________________

____

☐ I have something to say or questions to ask: ____________________

____

The Third Category: How does someone know when he or she should communicate to share ideas, thoughts, or feelings?

Communication is a good way to make connections with other people.

Sharing thoughts, feelings, and ideas from one mind to another is a way that people connect with one another. People do this by talking, listening, thinking about, and responding to thoughts, feelings, and ideas.

When family members, friends, teachers, therapists, and other important people ask questions about thoughts and feelings, it may be a good time to communicate by trying to answer the questions.

If it is difficult to answer at that time, a person can say, **"I'll try to answer these questions, but not right now. Let's find another time to talk about these things."** The time to talk about it may be written into the day's schedule or on the weekly calendar.

Sometimes another method of communication may be preferred instead of talking. Try having a "**Computer Conversation**" by sitting side by side at the computer and taking turns typing. Email may be another option.

Communication Form

☑ I will check what is true for me.

- ☐ I usually like to communicate my ideas and thoughts.
- ☐ I usually do not like to communicate my ideas and thoughts.
- ☐ I usually like to communicate my feelings.
- ☐ I usually do not like to communicate my feelings.
- ☐ I would sometimes like to communicate by writing instead of talking.

What are the most common methods of communication?

Communication can be verbal (talking and listening) or visual (writing and reading).

A person who has something to communicate can talk, write a letter with pen or pencil, or use a computer.

If it is written, it can be on paper, on the computer and printed out, or by email.

Some people communicate by gesturing with their hands. They may communicate using facial expressions and eye contact. Some people may use pictures or photographs to communicate.

The most common methods are talking and listening, writing and reading.

Communication Form

☑ I will check what is true for me.

☐ I will mark the words in the paragraph above that describe the ways I prefer to communicate.

☐ I do not know how I prefer to communicate.

☐ I have questions or something to say: ______________________________

____

What is other important information about communication?

Successful communication is done honestly and with respect. Both of these qualities (honesty and respect) are what make a successful communicator.

Being honest is saying what is true for oneself.

Being respectful is acting courteously and politely.

Communicating in a respectful manner is of utmost importance. Positive change is possible when communication is both honest and respectful. Connections with people may be strengthened when communication is both honest and respectful. More information can be found in Chapter 16.

Communication Form

☑ I will check what is true for me.

- ☐ I understand what it means to be honest.
- ☐ I do not understand what it means to be honest.
- ☐ I understand what it means to be respectful.
- ☐ I do not understand what it means to be respectful.
- ☐ I understand what it means to be courteous or polite.
- ☐ I do not understand what it means to be courteous or polite.
- ☐ I think that I am usually honest. I say what it true for me.
- ☐ I think that I am usually respectful. I usually am courteous and polite.
- ☐ I am not sure if I am usually both honest and respectful when I communicate.
- ☐ I would like more information about honesty, respect, and being polite.

If there is something that a person didn't communicate to someone who died, is it too late now?

Sometimes people wish that they had communicated with someone who has already died. They may have wanted to say "**thank you,**" but never did. They may have wanted to tell the person something else, but didn't.

Wise people teach that it is never too late to try to communicate, even if the person has already died. In this case, use the following **Communication Form** (on both pages) to make a plan.

Communication Form

☑ First, I will choose the best ideas for me. I prefer:

- ☐ To write a letter to the person who has died.
- ☐ To write a poem about what I want to say.
- ☐ To tell a family member or someone else what I want to say and ask them to write it down for me.
- ☐ To draw a picture while thinking of what I want to say.
- ☐ To say or write a prayer about what I want to say.
- ☐ To sit in a quiet place and talk to the person aloud or in my mind.
- ☐ To choose other way to communicate what I want to say. Other ways could be: ______________________________

  ____

  ____

☑ Next, I will choose one of these ways to deliver the communication:

☐ Place the letter, picture, poem, or other item in the casket with the body of the person who has died.

☐ Place the letter, picture, poem, or other item at the grave of the person who has died.

☐ Get someone to help me burn it in a fireplace, campfire, or other safe place. (Think of the smoke carrying the message to the person.)

☐ Put it in a special place at home, like under a favorite item, rock, picture, or home altar.

☐ Go to my church, temple, or place of worship, and read my message quietly.

☐ Go to my church, temple, or place of worship. Give it to the priest, rabbi, nun, monk, cleric, or other religious authority, and ask him or her to put it in a special place or include it in their prayers or meditations.

☐ Bury it or scatter it in nature, like in a garden, river, ocean, lake, woods, hill, meadow, desert, mountain, or somewhere else.

☐ Place it somewhere significant to the person who has died. I may place it:

____

____

☑ After delivering the communication, I can try to picture in my mind, the person receiving it.

CHAPTER 6: What Happens to the Person Who Dies

What does it mean that death is a "mystery"?

When something is a **mystery**, it means that it is difficult to understand or explain.

Death is considered a mystery because people throughout history have wondered about the purpose of death and what happens to a person after death.

Communication Form

☑ I will check what is true for me.

- ☐ I have never really thought much about death before reading this book.
- ☐ I have not thought much about death until a person or animal I knew died.
- ☐ I think about death sometimes.
- ☐ I wonder what happens to people after they die.
- ☐ I am not interested in thinking about what happens to people after they die.
- ☐ I have something to say or questions to ask: ____________________

  ____

What happens to the person after he or she dies?

This is probably the biggest mystery of life.

People know that when all the cells of the physical body stop functioning, the body dies. We know when the body of a person has died.

In most cases, the body of the person is taken care of in a respectful manner by family members, friends, doctors, funeral directors, or other people.

The physical body of the person is usually buried or cremated. (Information about burials and cremations can be found in Chapters 8 and 9.) However, many people believe that there is more to a person than the physical body.

Many people believe that there is an invisible part of the person who continues to live in the "afterlife." The term "afterlife" refers to the belief about life after death. There are many different beliefs about what happens to a person after death.

What do "belief" and "to believe in something" mean?

"To believe in something" means to feel, imagine, and/or know that something is true. A "belief" is something that people feel, imagine, and/or know to be true.

Beliefs do not have to be proven by science.

Individual people have different beliefs about the same subject.

Keep reading to find out about what some people believe happens after someone dies.

What are some beliefs about what happens to the person after death?

Here are four types of beliefs about what happens to a person after death.

1. Some people believe that once the body dies, it is the **end of that person** forever.

2. Other people believe that there are two parts that make up a person. One part is the "physical body" of the person, and the other part is the "soul" of the person.

The **physical body** is the part of the person that can be seen and touched. It is the part that dies at the end of the lifespan. It is buried or cremated.

The **soul** is the other part of the person. It is invisible. Some people say that they feel or sense the soul of the person after the person's body has died, but the soul cannot be seen. Sometimes people may use the word "spirit."

Different religions or spiritual paths teach about the soul of a person. Some people who do not follow a religion or spiritual path, also believe that people have a soul.

The physical body is sometimes compared to a shell. **Many people believe that the soul of the person separates from the body when the body dies.** It can be compared to a snail leaving its shell. After death, what we see is the "shell" or the body of the person. After death, the soul of the person is not in the body anymore.

Most religions and spiritual paths offer answers to questions about what happens to the soul when the body dies. For example, some teach that the soul returns to God or goes to heaven. Some teach that the soul returns to Earth by being born as another person. There are many other different beliefs about what happens to the soul after the person dies.

3. A third belief is that the life energy of the person doesn't really die, but that it continues on in other forms. **The energy that was the person, including the cells of the body and the mind of the person change form and live on**

in nature or in the universe. The belief is that life is constantly renewing, and never actually dies. This belief teaches that there really is no birth and death, only life changing form, on and on. The person is not the person anymore, but the life energy continues on.

4. The fourth belief is being unsure. **Some people are not sure what they believe about life after death.** They are not sure if they believe that people are only their physical bodies, or if they believe that people have a soul, too.

What happens after death is considered a mystery. People have different beliefs about what happens after death.

Communication Form

☑ I will check what is true for me.

☐ I have a religion. It is ____.

☐ I want to know what my religion teaches about what happens after death.

☐ I do not have a religion.

☐ I have a spiritual path or spiritual practice. It is ____________________

____

☐ I want to know what my spiritual practice teaches about what happens after death.

☐ I am not sure if I have a religion or spiritual practice.

☐ My family believes that after someone dies, this happens:______________

____

☐ I have something to say or questions to ask:________________________

____

Most People Agree On One Thing

No matter what people believe about what happens to a person after he or she dies, most people agree on this:

When the people who are alive here on Earth **remember** the person who has died, the person "lives on." This means that the person who died "is still alive" in the memories of the people who remember him or her.

"Remembering a person" includes thinking about, talking about, hearing about, or doing special things related to the person who has died. Chapters 8, 10, 11, and 12 give more information about special things that people may do or say to keep the person alive in their memories.

Communication Form

☑ I will check what is true for me.

- ☐ I remember someone who has died. His or her name is ______________
- ☐ Sometimes I think about him or her.
- ☐ Some memories of the person are______________________________

  ____
- ☐ I want to think about him or her, now.
- ☐ I want to talk about him or her, now.
- ☐ I want to listen to someone else talk about him or her, now.
- ☐ I do not want to think about him or her, right now.
- ☐ I may want to think about him or her in the future.
- ☐ I may want to talk about, or hear about, him or her in the future.
- ☐ I have something to say or questions to ask: ______________________

☐ Here are some of my questions or thoughts about the information in this chapter. I do not have to fill in all these lines. I will only write what I want to ask or to say: ____________________

CHAPTER 7: Putting Pets To Sleep

What does it mean when a pet has to be "put to sleep"?

Sometimes dogs or cats or other pets become very sick. Or they are very very old.

An animal might not be able to walk or eat, or it may be feeling a lot of pain. It may make sounds, or it may be very quiet. The veterinarian may think that the animal is hurting inside its body.

The veterinarian may understand that the animal will never get better again; that the animal is dying.

Sometimes the most helpful thing to do for an animal that is loved by its family is to "put him or her to sleep." This is the term used to describe the way the veterinarian and family members help animals die peacefully when they are coming close to the end of their lifespan.

"Putting an animal to sleep" does not mean that it is going to sleep in the usual way. It will not really sleep and wake up. An animal that has been "put to sleep" in this way does not wake up.

It does not hurt the animal to be "put to sleep." It is usually considered to be a humane and compassionate way to help animals die easily and without pain. It is a legal method performed by veterinarians using special drugs and injections. It takes only minutes for the animal to die peacefully. Another name for this is "euthanasia."

Communication Form

☑ I will check what is true for me.

☐ An animal or several animals are a part of our family. The names and ages of the animals are: ______________________________

____

____

☐ I know an animal (or animals) who have died. Their names and the dates of their deaths are: ______________________________

____

____

☐ I have never had a pet who has died.

☐ I wonder if our pet is sick or injured.

☐ I wonder if our pet may die soon.

☐ I wonder if we will help our pet die peacefully by having the veterinarian put him or her to sleep.

☐ I want to talk with a trusted person and/or the veterinarian about this.

☐ I have something to say or questions to ask: ______________________________

____

Do doctors put people "to sleep" in the same way as veterinarians put animals "to sleep"?

No, generally they do not. Most people in the world die naturally because of old age, illness, or accidents.

Once in a while a person who has been dying for a long time feels lots of pain. There may be no medicine or treatment that relieves the severe pain. The person may ask the doctor to prescribe the drugs that will cause unconsciousness and cause the body to stop functioning, making death happen soon.

All doctors, families, religions, and government officials do not agree on whether this should be a choice for humans. Most people agree that it is different for animals. It is common for veterinarians to help animals die peacefully.

Doctors giving people drugs to cause death in this way is rare. It is illegal in many parts of the world. Euthanasia for people is controversial. This means that many people have strong feelings about it.

Some people feel strongly that euthanasia should be a choice for people who are dying and in severe pain.

Other people feel strongly that it is wrong to help someone die in this way. Some religions have strong opinions on euthanasia.

Some people become very upset by this topic. Some people may not want to talk about it at all.

If a person has questions or opinions about euthanasia, he or she should talk with family members or others about it at home, privately, and at a time when a person who is sick and/or dying is not present. Talking about it privately is polite and respectful.

Euthanasia is a topic that may be upsetting for some people to hear about or to talk about.

Communication Form

☑ I will check what is true for me.

- ☐ I wonder about my family's opinion on euthanasia. I have something to say or questions to ask. My questions are: ______________________

  ____

  ____

- ☐ If I have a religion, I wonder what our religious beliefs are about this topic.

- ☐ I want to talk with a priest, minister, pastor, rabbi, cleric, teacher, or other religious offical about this topic.

- ☐ I have a question about euthanasia.

- ☐ I have an opinion about euthanasia.

- ☐ I do not have an opinion about euthanasia.

- ☐ I want to talk with someone about euthanasia. The person or people I want to talk with are ______________________

  ____

- ☐ I have something to say or questions to ask: ______________________

  ____

Chapter 8: Rituals and Traditions

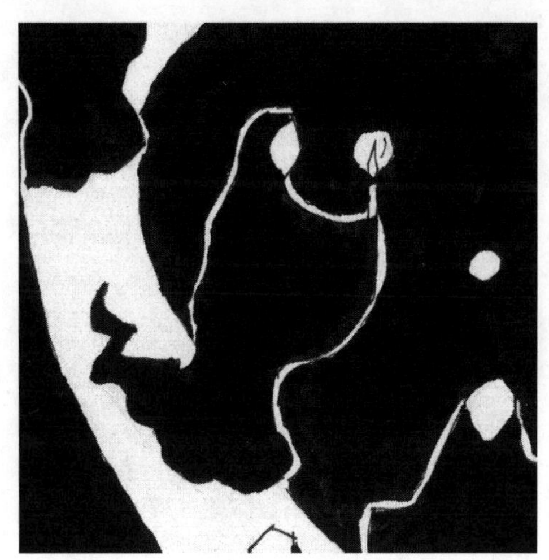

What rituals and traditions are practiced after someone has died?

"Rituals" are particular things that people do to mark an important event.

After someone has died, people often participate in a ritual. Participating in rituals can help the living people get used to the fact that something has ended (the life of a person or animal) and something different is now beginning (living without that person or animal here in the physical world). Sometimes families make up special rituals after a person or animal has died.

Some people believe that the purpose of a particular ritual is to help the soul of the person who has died.

"Traditions" are rituals that have been done the same way for many years. Most religions have traditions to mark different events. Most religions have specific traditions to follow after someone dies.

Traditions after death in one religion, or culture, or country in the world may be very different from those in another religion, culture, or country. This book describes some common rituals or traditions practiced in some cultures or countries. There are other rituals or traditions that may not be described in this book.

Communication Form

☑ I will check what is true for me.

- ☐ I live in this country: ______________________________
- ☐ I am a part of a specific culture. It is______________________________
- ☐ I have a religion. It is ______________________________
- ☐ I do not have a religion.
- ☐ I (or my family and culture) follow specific traditions after someone dies.
- ☐ We choose our own ritual after someone dies.
- ☐ We probably will not do a ritual after a person dies.
- ☐ I want to find out what we will do after a person dies.
- ☐ I have something to say or questions to ask:______________________

____

____

What is a "wake" or a "viewing"?

A common ritual or tradition following a death of a person in some cultures is to have a "wake" or a "viewing." If there is one, it usually happens soon after the person has died.

This is when family members and friends come together to visit with each other, to comfort each other, and to sometimes see the body of the person who has died.

If the word "viewing" is used, it means that the body of the person who has died can be viewed, or seen.

A wake or viewing may take place at a funeral home, a person's home, or in another building. There may be flowers on display. If there are only a few people and they are talking quietly, the room is usually quiet. If there are a lot of people, or if the people are talking loudly, the room may be noisy.

The body of the person who has died may be lying in a casket. It might look like he or she is sleeping, but everyone knows that is not the case. It is true that the person has died.

Some people stand for a few minutes at the casket to look at the person's body. Some people say goodbye to the person. Some people write a note or draw a picture to place with the body. Often, children write notes or draw pictures to place with the body.

It is safe and okay to touch the body. The body feels different than usual, because it is not alive anymore.

Sometimes close family members may kiss or hug the body when they are saying goodbye. This is okay.

At the wake, people usually try to talk quietly, although some people may talk loudly. Some people may cry. Sometimes people laugh, especially when they remember good times they had with the person in the past.

Photographs of the person may be displayed. Sometimes the photographs show the person at different ages with family and friends.

Sometimes the casket is closed. This means that the person's body is in the casket, but it cannot be seen. This is okay.

It is okay to ask questions about the person, about the body, about the casket, and about what is happening.

Sometimes parents have their children stay at home when there is a wake, or sometimes children go to the wake.

Communication Form

☑ I will check what is true for me.

- ☐ I know someone who has died. His or her name: ____________________
- ☐ There will be *(or was)* a wake or viewing.
- ☐ I am going *(or already went)* to the wake or viewing.
- ☐ Location of the wake or viewing: ____________________
- ☐ If I have a choice about going, I want to go to the wake.
- ☐ If I have a choice about going, I do not want to go to the wake.
- ☐ I want more information before going.
- ☐ I will underline or highlight the descriptions on the previous page that described *(or will describe)* this wake or viewing.
- ☐ I have something to say, or questions to ask: ____________________

  ____

  ____

What is a closed casket, and an open casket?

A casket is a large box made of wood, metal, or another material. In many cultures, the body of the person who has died is laid in a casket. There may be a pillow, sheet, or blanket in the casket.

Sometimes the casket is open. This is what is meant by the term "open casket."

The casket is open in case people who knew the person want to see the body of the person one more time. Sometimes people say goodbye to the person when they see the body in the casket. Sometimes people put special things, notes or letters, or other items in the casket to be buried with the body of the person.

The body of the person does not have life in it anymore, so the person will look different than when he or she was alive. Sometimes it looks like the person is sleeping, but he or she is not really sleeping. The life left the body when the person died. Only people who are alive can really go to sleep and wake up afterwards.

Some people who come to the wake or the funeral may gently touch or kiss the body of the person in the casket. It is okay to touch the body in a casket.

The body of the person who died is not alive. It feels different. It feels hard and the skin feels cold. Some people will touch it. Some people do not want to touch it. This is okay, too.

When the casket is closed, and the person cannot be seen, it is called a "closed casket." Some religious traditions or some families decide to keep the casket closed. This is okay. People can still say goodbye to the person when they see the closed casket.

If it is a closed casket, people can still write notes or have items placed in the casket. The casket can be opened later, and the things may be placed in the casket.

Communication Form

☑ I will check what is true for me.

- ☐ The person's body was *(is)* in a casket.
- ☐ The person's body was not *(is not)* in a casket.
- ☐ The casket was *(is going to be)* closed.
- ☐ The casket was *(is going to be)* open.
- ☐ I want to look in the casket.
- ☐ I want (name) ____________ to stand near me when I look in the casket.
- ☐ I may want to touch the body in the casket.
- ☐ I do not want to look in the casket.
- ☐ I do not want to look in it now, but I want someone to take a photograph of the casket, in case I want to see it sometime in the future.
- ☐ I want to write a note to be placed in the casket.
- ☐ I want to put something else in the casket:__________________________
- ☐ I want someone else to put my note or item in the casket.
- ☐ I have something to say, or questions to ask: ________________________

____

____

What is a funeral service?

Generally there is a funeral service after someone has died. If there was a wake or viewing, the funeral usually happens afterwards, within the next few days.

Friends and family members usually gather together for funerals. There may be a few people or there may be many people.

Funerals are generally held at a church, temple, or other religious building, but they can be held in other locations, too. They may be held outside.

Usually the casket with the body of the person who has died is at the funeral. There may be prayers and a religious service. Certain people may give speeches. There may be music and singing.

Some people may cry or laugh during or after the funeral. If there is a speech, sometimes the speakers share happy or funny memories of the person who has died. Sometimes this makes people think of the person and feel good, and they may laugh.

After the funeral, some people may go to the cemetery where the body of the person will be buried in a special place, called the "grave."

Family members and friends may get together to eat lunch or dinner after the funeral.

Many times, relatives and friends who live far away come for the funeral. They may not have seen each other in a long time. Even though they are sad that the person has died, they may also be happy to see each other. They may talk about many different things, since they haven't seen each other in a long time.

Sometimes parents have their children stay at home instead of going to the funeral. Sometimes the children go to the funeral.

It is okay to ask questions about the person who has died, about the body, about the casket, and what is happening.

Communication Form

☑ I will check what is true for me.

- ☐ I know someone who has died recently.
- ☐ There is going to be *(or was)* a funeral service.
- ☐ I am going *(or went)* to the funeral service.
- ☐ The location: ____
- ☐ If I have a choice, I want to go to the funeral.
- ☐ If it is possible, I would like to read something aloud or give a speech at the funeral.
- ☐ These are the people who will give a speech *(who gave a speech)* at the funeral: ____

  ____
- ☐ If I have a choice, I do not want to go to the funeral.
- ☐ I will underline or highlight the words on the previous page that describe the funeral that I attended *(will attend)*.
- ☐ I have questions or something to say: ________________________

  ____

What is a graveside service?

If the body is to be buried at a cemetery, there may be a graveside service, immediately following the funeral service. Some people will go to the cemetery where the grave is located.

The grave is the actual place where the person's body will be buried. If the person was cremated, the "cremains" may be buried in the grave. In some cultures, the cremains are kept in a special container in a shrine at the cemetery.

(More information about burials and cremations are in Chapter 9.)

Sometimes the cemetery is located within walking distance of the church, although most of the time people drive to the cemetery.

Often, cars are driven to the cemetery in a line with their headlights on. This is called a "funeral procession." The first car may be a "hearse," which is a special vehicle designed to carry the casket to the cemetery. Some family members may also ride in the hearse.

At the cemetery, the casket is taken to the grave. Usually prayers are said. If the person who has died served in the military, there may be a special service giving a flag to a relative. Sometimes people place flowers on the casket. Sometimes people place a handful of dirt on the casket, depending on the tradition that is being followed.

In some cultures, the cemetery is the place where the family shrine is located. It is a special place to keep the cremains of family members.

After the graveside service, family members and friends may eat lunch or dinner together at someone's house, or at a restaurant.

It is okay to ask questions about the person who has died, about the body, about the casket, about the grave, about the cemetery, and what is happening.

Communication Form

☑ I will check what is true for me.

- ☐ I know someone who has died recently.
- ☐ There is going to be *(or was)* a graveside service.
- ☐ I am going *(or went)* to the graveside service.
- ☐ Location ____ .
- ☐ If I have a choice, I want to go to the cemetery.
- ☐ If I have a choice, I do not want to go to the cemetery.
- ☐ Afterwards, I may underline or highlight the words on the previous page that describe the graveside service.
- ☐ I have something to say or questions to ask: ______________________

  ____

What is a memorial service?

There might be a memorial service. It is sometimes simply called a "memorial." The word "memory" is the root word of "memorial."

Friends and family members usually gather together for memorial services to remember the person who has died—to keep the person in their memories. There may be a few people or there may be many people.

The memorial may be at a church, temple, other religious building, another building, at a home, or outside in nature. It may take place a few days after the death, a few months later, or a year later. Some religious traditions hold memorial services several times during the year after the death, and again at special times in the future.

The body of the person who has died is not at the memorial service. The body usually has already been buried or cremated.

Similar to a funeral, there may be prayers, religious rituals, speeches, songs, music, or other special presentations.

Afterwards, people will talk with one another. People may laugh. People may cry. They may remember and talk about the good times they had with the person who has died.

Many times, relatives and friends who live far away come to memorial services. They may be happy to see each other. They may talk about many different things, since they haven't seen each other in a long time.

Sometimes there will be food to eat after the memorial, or people may go to someone's house or to a restaurant to eat together.

Sometimes children stay at home instead of going to a memorial service. Sometimes children go to the memorial service.

Communication Form

☑ I will check what is true for me.

☐ I know someone who has died, and there is going to be a memorial service for him or her.

☐ Date of the memorial service:______________________________

☐ Location of the memorial service: ____________________________

☐ I am going *(or already went)* to the memorial service.

☐ If I have a choice, I want to go to the memorial service.

☐ If it is possible, I want to read something aloud, or give a speech at the memorial.

☐ These are the people who are going to give a speech *(gave a speech)* at the memorial: ____

____

☐ If I have a choice, I do not want to go to the memorial.

☐ I will underline or highlight the sentences on the previous page that describe the memorial service.

☐ I have something to say or questions to ask:______________________

____

What is a "celebration of life" for someone who has died?

Sometimes people choose to have a "celebration of life" to honor someone who has died. The term "celebration of life" is used to remind people to "celebrate" the life of the person who died.

"Celebrations of life" are similar to "memorial services." The same description on the previous pages for a memorial service also describes a celebration of life.

People think about the person and about how much they loved and enjoyed the person. They think about and talk about what the person was like, what they did, and other memories they have of the person.

Communication Form

☑ I will check what is true for me.

☐ I know someone who has died and there is going to be a "celebration of life" for him or her.

☐ Date of the celebration: ____________________

☐ Location of the celebration: ____________________

☐ I am going *(or went)* to the celebration.

☐ If I have a choice, I want to go to the celebration.

☐ If it is possible, I want to read something aloud, or give a speech at the celebration of life.

☐ If I have a choice, I do not want to go.

☐ I have something to say or questions to ask: ____________________

____

What happens when people come to a family member's home after a service?

Sometimes after a service, people are invited to the home of a family member. It may be my family's home or another home.

Many people are comforted by being together after a funeral or other service.

People often bring food to share. There will be talking and visiting and eating. There may be a lot of activity and noise.

I may want to talk or play with the visitors. I may want to be by myself for a while. It is okay to find a quiet place to be when many people come to a house after a wake, funeral, memorial, or celebration of life.

Communication Form

☑ I will check what is true for me.

- ☐ I am going to *(or went)* to someone's house after a service.
- ☐ People are coming *(or came)* to my house after a service.
- ☐ People are going *(or went)* to someone else's house after a service.
- ☐ I want to play with or talk with others, at the house. *(I played and talked with others at the house.)*
- ☐ I would like to be in the same room with others, but I want to read or play by myself. *(I was in the same room with others, but I stayed to myself.)*
- ☐ I would like to be in a quiet room by myself. I can tell my parents or a trusted person when I want to be alone. *(I went to a quiet room by myself.)*
- ☐ I will underline or highlight the sentences on the previous page that describe the gathering of people at the house.
- ☐ I have something to say or questions to ask: ______________________

Chapter 9: Taking Care of the Physical Body

What happens to the body after dying?

There are special ways that people take care of the body after someone dies.

The body may be washed and prepared in a special way. Sometimes a professional funeral director takes care of the body. Sometimes family members and close friends take care of the body.

In some cultures, the body is dressed like the person would be dressed as if he or she were still alive. In some cultures, the body is wrapped in a special cloth, called a "shroud." Or the person may be dressed, and also covered with a shroud.

In some cultures, the body is placed in a casket. The casket may be open or it may be closed. The casket may be present during one of the services mentioned in Chapter 8. If the body is to be buried, it will be taken to a cemetery. If the body is to be cremated, it is taken to where the cremation will be performed.

On rare occasions the body is to be "donated to science." This means that the body will be taken and cared for by a university medical school or another scientific institution.

There is more information in this chapter about cemeteries, burials, cremation, and donating to science.

What is a shroud?

In some cultures or countries the body is wrapped in a shroud, which is a special cloth for this purpose. The body wrapped in a shroud may be placed in a casket. Or the shroud may cover the body, like a blanket. In some cultures, the body is wrapped in a shroud and carried or placed on a special table or on the ground.

Communication Form

☑ I will check what is true for me.

- ☐ I know a person who has died.
- ☐ The body was cared for by a professional funeral director.
- ☐ The body was cared for by family or friends.
- ☐ The body was placed in a casket.
- ☐ The body was wrapped in a shroud.
- ☐ The body was covered with a shroud, like a blanket.
- ☐ The body was buried.
- ☐ The body was cremated.
- ☐ The body was donated to science.
- ☐ I have something to say or questions to ask: ______________________

____

____

What does it mean for the body to be buried?

When a body is to be buried, a deep hole is dug in the ground.

In many cultures, the hole is located at a cemetery. Usually it is the job of the people who work at the cemetery to dig the hole. In some cultures, family or friends may dig the hole. The hole may be dug with shovels, or by a machine. The casket with the body inside is placed in the deep hole and covered with dirt. Or, the body wrapped in a shroud may be placed directly into the deep hole and covered with dirt.

Sometimes family members and friends place flowers or handfuls of dirt on top of the casket as a way of saying goodbye and helping to bury the body.

The place where the body is buried is called the "grave." Sometimes there is a "gravestone" which is a special large stone to mark the grave. The name of the person with the year of birth and the year of death is often carved on the gravestone, although the dates may not be carved into the stone at the time of the funeral yet. Sometimes gravestones are placed at the grave later on.

The name and dates are carved in the gravestone so that family members, friends, and future generations will be able to locate the grave in the cemetery.

In some countries, the family returns to the cemetery a few years after the burial to take care of the bones. After a few years, the soft tissues of the body have returned to the Earth, and the bones are left. The bones are taken out of the grave, cleaned, and anointed with special oil and taken to a special place in a church or other holy place. There, they are kept with the bones of other family members.

The body that is buried is not alive. It cannot feel pain or other physical sensations anymore. Life already left the body when the person died.

Communication Form

☑ I will check what is true for me.

☐ I know a person who has died. His or her name is:_______________

☐ The person's body is going to be *(or was)* buried.

☐ The body was cremated and the cremains are going to be *(or were)* buried.

☐ I am going *(or went)* to the grave.

☐ I am not going *(or did not go)* to the grave.

☐ Location of the grave: _______________

☐ Date of the burial: _______________

☐ I have something to say or questions to ask:_______________

____

____

What is a cemetery?

A cemetery is a special place where the bodies of people may be buried after they die. Remains of the bodies which have been cremated ("cremains") may be buried there, also.

Another word for cemetery is "graveyard."

In some places, families have their own graveyard where the bodies or the cremains of their ancestors have been buried for many generations.

Sometimes families have their own section in a cemetery.

In some cultures, family "shrines" are located in cemeteries. The cremains of family members are located in the family shrines, at the cemetery.

Cemeteries are located in or near most towns or cities.

The graves are generally marked by gravestones (also called "tombstones") usually showing the person's name and dates of the birth and death.

Sometimes people enjoy taking walks in cemeteries because they are quiet and peaceful places.

Communication Form

☑ I will check what is true for me.

- ☐ I have been to a cemetery. Name of cemetery: ____________________

  ____

- ☐ Some of the things I saw at the cemetery were:____________________

  ____

- ☐ I went to the cemetery to visit the grave of____________________ .
- ☐ I went to a cemetery to take a quiet walk.
- ☐ I have not been to a cemetery.
- ☐ I would like to take a walk in a cemetery.
- ☐ I would not like to walk through a cemetery.
- ☐ I (or my family) know people who have died, whose bodies have been buried at a cemetery.
- ☐ I (or my family) know people who have died, whose cremains are kept in a shrine at a cemetery.
- ☐ I have something to say or questions to ask:____________________

  ____

  ____

What are tombs, crypts, and mausoleums?

These are words that describe other places to keep the bodies of people who have died.

A "tomb" is another word for the place of burial. It may be in the ground, like a grave, or it may be in a crypt.

A "crypt" is the container that can be used to store the body of a person who has died. It is usually built out of stone or concrete, and is located above the ground. Crypts are usually located in buildings called mausoleums.

A "mausoleum" is a building where tombs can be kept above ground, instead of buried in the Earth. Mausoleums are often located in cemeteries. They are sometimes located in churches or other religious buildings, public buildings, or elsewhere.

The body that is in a tomb, crypt, or mausoleum is not alive. It cannot feel pain or other physical sensations, anymore. Life has already left the body.

Communication Form

☑ I will check what is true for me.

☐ I knew someone whose body is kept in a crypt in a mausoleum. His or her name is ______________________________

☐ I have visited a mausoleum. Location: ______________________

☐ I saw the outside of a crypt for (name) ______________________

☐ The dates on the crypt were: ______________________________

☐ I have not visited a mausoleum.

☐ I have something to say or questions to ask: ________________

____

What does it mean to be "buried at sea"?

In some cultures on islands or coastal areas, the body may be "buried at sea."

In these cases, the body is taken out to sea and allowed to drift to the bottom.

The body that is buried at sea is not alive. It cannot feel pain or other physical sensations anymore. Life already left the body when the person died.

Communication Form

☑ I will check what is true for me.

- ☐ I live in an area of the world where bodies are sometimes buried at sea.
- ☐ I do not live in an area where bodies are buried at sea.
- ☐ We know someone whose body is going to be *(or has been)* buried at sea. His or her name is ______________________________
- ☐ Date of the burial at sea: ______________________________
- ☐ I have something to say or questions to ask: ______________________________

____

____

What does it mean for the body to be cremated?

When a body is to be cremated, it is taken to a special place called a "crematorium." There, the body is put into a large chamber and heated until it turns to ash.

In some cultures, the cremation happens outside in a special fire.

What is left of the body after a cremation is called "cremains." Sometimes the cremains are mostly ashes. Sometimes the cremains are a mixture of ashes and bones. The cremains usually are saved and given to a family member.

The body that is cremated is not alive. It cannot feel pain or other physical sensations anymore. Life already left the body when the person died.

What happens to the cremains?

Sometimes family members keep the cremains in a special container at home.

Sometimes the cremains are kept in a special place called a "shrine" which may be located in a cemetery or another special place.

Sometimes the cremains are buried in a cemetery.

Sometimes family members and friends spread the cremains in a special location, like the ocean or the mountains, or at a favorite place of the person who has died.

Communication Form

☑ I will check what is true for me.

- ☐ We know someone whose body will be *(or has been)* cremated. His or her name is: ______________________________
- ☐ The cremains will be *(or are)* in a special container.
- ☐ I have seen the container.
- ☐ I have not seen the container.
- ☐ I want to see the container.
- ☐ The cremains will be *(or are)* buried.
- ☐ The cremains will be *(or are)* kept in a shrine.
- ☐ The cremains will be *(or have been)* spread in a special place. The special place is______________________________
- ☐ I have questions or something to say: ______________________________

____

____

What does it mean for the body to be donated to science?

Bodies "donated to science" are used to educate students who are learning to be medical doctors, chiropractors, nurses, physical therapists, and others who are studying science and medical professions. The bodies are used to help students learn about the physical body.

Some people want to help science in this way. When they are alive, they may decide that when they die, the body is to be "donated to science."

To do this, people must sign a contract with a medical institution before they die. The medical institution agrees ahead of time to take care of the body after the person dies.

In medical institutions, the body is handled in a respectful manner.

After students have finished learning about the body, it is cremated.

The body that is donated to science and later cremated is not alive. It cannot feel pain or other physical sensations anymore. Life already left the body when the person died.

Communication Form

☑ I will check what is true for me.

☐ I (or my family) know someone whose body will be *(or was)* donated to science. His or her name is ______________________________

☐ The name of the medical institution is ______________________________

____

☐ We do not know the name of the medical institution.

☐ I have something to say or questions to ask: ______________________________

____

____

Does being cremated, buried, kept in a mausoleum, or being donated to science, hurt the person who has died?

The person is not hurt by the body being buried or cremated. The person is not hurt if the body is kept in a mausoleum. The person is not hurt if the body is donated to science.

After a person dies, the body stops functioning. Life leaves the body. Because the life is gone from every part of the body, the person cannot feel physical sensation.

If the person had been sick or in pain before dying, they now are not sick or in pain anymore. They do not feel physical pain and they do not feel hurt the way people do when they are alive.

Burial and cremation are traditions that have been performed since ancient times. Life has already left the body before it is buried, cremated, or donated to science.

Who decides what to do with the body?

Before they die, some people tell family members and friends what to do with their body after they die. It is called "telling people your wishes."

The person may have requested that his or her body be cremated. The person may have requested that his or her body be buried. The person may have signed a contract with a medical institution to have the body donated to science after death.

It is the responsibility of family members and friends to try to follow the person's wishes to the best of their abilities.

When they are still alive, people may make choices about the type of funeral or memorial service they want. They may choose the music, songs, prayers, or other things to be read. They might choose where they want their body to be buried or where they want their cremains to be spread.

It is helpful if people write down their wishes ahead of time, about what they want to have happen to their body after they die, so their family members and friends will know what to do.

In the cases where no one knows what the person wanted to have done with his or her body or what kind of services were desired, the decision is usually made by family members and close friends. They try to imagine what the person would have wanted.

Sometimes a person's religious tradition will determine what happens to the body after death.

Some religions prescribe that the body should be cremated. Some religions prescribe that the body should be buried.

Communication Form

☑ I will check what is true for me.

☐ I (or my family) knows someone who has died.

☐ The person who died had a religion or spiritual tradition determine what happens to the body after dying. The religion or spiritual tradition is: ___

___

☐ The person had communicated his or her "wishes" before dying.

☐ I have something to say or questions to ask: ___

___

___

CHAPTER 10: What People Say and Do

What do people say after someone has died?

Living people may feel sad when someone has died. They may be comforted by hearing kind words said by other people who care. They may also be comforted by receiving cards or letters that have been sent to them.

Saying or writing comforting words is a kind thing to do.

Most cultures have certain words or phrases that are typically said at this time. Below is a list of phrases that are often said by people when someone has died.

Underline the ones that you have heard. Add other phrases to this list that may be said by people in your family, culture, country, or religious tradition.

(Some examples on this list use the pronoun "he" and some examples use the pronoun "she." These phrases are examples. In real life, use "he" or "she" depending on whether the person who died is male or female.)

- He is at peace.
- She is in Heaven now.
- He lived a long good life.
- She is with the angels.
- He is with us in spirit.
- She is in a better place.
- May her memory be eternal.
- He is with the ancestors.
- I will always remember him.
- I will light a candle for her.
- I will pray for him.
- I will pray for you.
- I am sorry for your loss.
- We will miss her.
- We were lucky to know him.
- He lived a short but full life.

- She is not suffering anymore. *(May be said when the person had been very sick for a long time before dying.)*
- May he rest in peace.
- She lived a full life.
- Life to you.
- Life to us.
- Other: ______________________________

In order to be comforting, a person must say something that is both kind and truthful.

Even gently saying, **"I don't know what to say,"** may be comforting to a person who has lost a loved one, if it is said kindly. Sometimes not saying anything while standing near someone or sitting quietly next to someone is comforting. Sometimes giving the person a hug or a gentle touch on the back may be comforting.

Writing kind and honest words in a card, and mailing it may also be comforting to a person whose family member or friend has died.

Communication Form

☑ I will check what is true for me.

☐ I want to say something comforting to (name)____________________

☐ I do not want to say anything at this time to (name) ______________

☐ I want help in choosing what to say.

☐ This is what I plan to say ______________________________

☐ I want to write a card or note to______________________________

☐ I have questions or something to say:___________________________

____

What should I say if someone tries to say "comforting words" to me?

Saying "yes" or "thank you" is an appropriate and polite response.

What if someone tries to touch, hug, or kiss me at this time?

Depending on the culture; touching, hugging, and kissing may be customary with family members or close friends. These behaviors may happen frequently at funerals and memorial services.

Many people are comforted by touches or hugs after someone has died, because hugging helps them feel close to others.

Adults who are family members or friends may want to hug or hold a child; it is their way of trying to be comforting.

It is okay to accept hugs while in a group of people at memorial services or funerals after someone has died.

Sometimes children or teenagers or adults may feel uncomfortable with hugs or kisses. If this is too uncomfortable, it is okay to say **"Thank you, but please don't hug (kiss) me."**

An intelligent way to say this is in a kind and polite manner. At funerals or memorial services, the intent of the hugger is to be kind, so try to speak kindly and politely when refusing hugs or kisses.

Some cultures have the custom of bowing, or other styles of physical interaction, instead of hugging.

Communication Form

☑ I will check what is true for me.

- ☐ Someone hugged or touched me at a funeral or other service.
- ☐ Someone kissed me at a funeral or other service.
- ☐ The name of the person or people who hugged, touched, or kissed me, or wanted to hug, touch, or kiss me were (names) ____________________ .

  ____

  ____

- ☐ I was comfortable being hugged, touched, or kissed at that time.
- ☐ I did not want to be hugged, touched, or kissed.
- ☐ I wanted to be hugged, touched, or kissed by some people, but not others.
- ☐ I wanted to give someone a hug. I wanted to hug (name)______________
- ☐ I gave someone a hug. I hugged (name) ____________________________
- ☐ In my culture, we generally use another style of interaction instead of hugging and kissing. The way of interaction at these times in my culture is to ____

  ____

- ☐ I have questions to ask or something to say: _______________________

  ____

  ____

CHAPTER 11: Taking Care of the Soul: More Rituals and Traditions

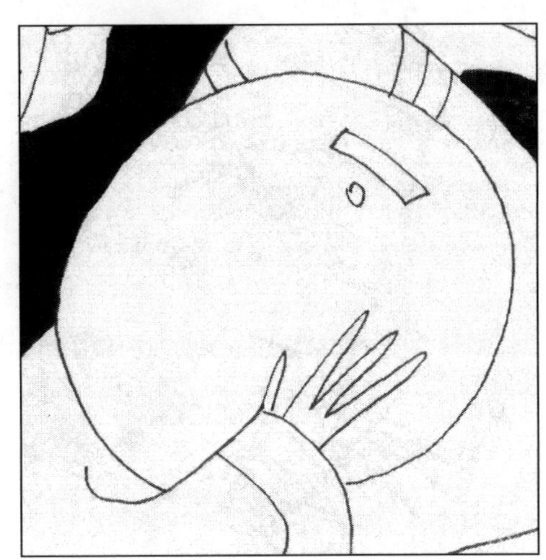

Why do people visit the grave, shrine, or keep the cremains of the person who has died?

Many people want to remember the person who has died, even though they cannot see the person anymore.

They like to find time to be quiet and think about the person who has died.

They may like to sit quietly at the grave or visit the shrine while they think of the person, talk to them in their mind, ask for help, or pray for them.

Doing these things may help people feel better when they miss a person or animal who has died.

Visiting the grave, shrine, or seeing the container of cremains helps them feel connected to the person who has died.

Communication Form

☑ I will check what is true for me.

☐ I have visited the grave or shrine of a person who has died.

☐ I want to visit the grave or shrine of (name) ____________________

☐ I do not want to visit the grave or shrine.

☐ I want to see the container of cremains.

☐ I do not want to see the container of cremains.

☐ Sometimes I think about the person who died.

☐ Sometimes I do not think about the person who died.

☐ I have something to say or questions to ask: ____________________

____

____

Why do people sometimes do special things to remember the person who has died?

According to some religious traditions and spiritual practices, remembering the person who has died is a way to help the soul of the person who has died. Doing something special in their memory is considered an important way to take care of their soul.

Rituals may be performed to help people take time to remember and think about a person who has died.

Some people write poems or essays, sing songs, or draw pictures while thinking of the person. Some people think of the person while they are dancing. Some people sit quietly and think about the person.

Some people go outdoors in nature and think of the person. They may take a walk. They look at the grass, trees, flowers, insects, squirrels, clouds, rivers, lakes, or ocean and remember the person. Some people sit around a campfire or look at a candle flame, and think about and talk about the person.

There are many ways to take time in daily life to remember a person or animal who has died. It is also okay just to think of the person or animal quietly without doing anything special or different.

Does everyone have to participate in a special ritual for someone who has died?

Some families want their children and other family members to participate in a ritual for someone who has died. Everyone in the family is there together.

In some families, it is a choice. If there is a choice, each person can make the decision for him or herself. The person may choose "yes" to participate in the ritual, or the person may choose "no"—not to participate in the ritual.

Communication Form

☑ I will check what is true for me.

☐ I am interested in participating in a special ritual for (name) __________

☐ I am not interested in a special ritual for (name) ________________

☐ I am not sure about participating in a special ritual. I want more information before deciding.

☐ This is my family's plan for the special ritual: ____________________

____

☐ I want to invent my own special ritual for the person or animal who died.

☐ I have a question or something to say: ________________________

____

____

If I want to create a special ritual for a person or animal who has died, what might I do?

Here is a list of ideas. Family members and friends may have other ideas.

There is no right way or wrong way to perform a ritual for a person or animal who died. It is good to enjoy memories of the person. It is okay to have fun while remembering the person! Some ideas are:

- Put flowers in a vase next to a picture of the person or animal.
- Plant flower bulbs in the fall to bloom in the spring.
- Plant a favorite flower of the person.
- Plant a perennial so it comes up every year.
- Say a prayer for the person's soul.
- Draw a picture.
- Light a candle.
- Write a story or a poem about the person or animal.
- Wear an article of clothing or jewelry that belonged to the person, like a pair of gloves, a shirt, a hat, or a piece of jewelry.
- Go for a walk in nature while thinking of the person or animal.
- Sit quietly in nature while thinking of the person or animal.
- Go for a walk in the neighborhood while thinking of the person or animal.
- Sing a song while thinking of the person or animal.
- Do a dance while thinking of the person or animal.
- Plant a tree in memory of the person or animal.
- Burn some incense and pray.
- Visit the person's grave or shrine.
- Ring a bell while thinking of the person or animal.
- Put a photograph of the person or animal in a special frame.
- Play music or a special song, and think of him/her.
- Play music, or a song, that the person liked.
- Hang a wind chime outside. Think of the person or animal when it rings.

- Bake a cake while thinking of the person or animal. Share it with someone else who wants to remember him/her.
- Cook the person's favorite food for dinner or lunch.
- Donate money to a charity in honor of the person. Choose a charity that supports something the person believed it.
- Write a story, poem, essay, article, or book, and dedicate it to the memory of the person or animal.
- Try to follow good and positive advice that the person believed in.
- Other: ____

Communication Form

☑ I will check what is true for me.

☐ I would like to do something special in memory of the person or animal who died. I will underline or highlight my favorite ideas from the list.

☐ I would like someone to help me plan a special ritual. The person I want to help me is (name) ______________________________

☐ I would like to invite other people to be with me for the special ritual. These are the people I want to invite:

____

____

☐ I would like to perform a ritual in memory of the person who died, by myself.

☐ I do not want to perform a ritual in memory of the person who died.

☐ I might want to perform a ritual sometime later, but not soon.

☐ I have something to say or questions to ask: ______________________

____

When should I perform a ritual for a person or animal who has died?

Rituals can be performed anytime. Sometimes rituals are performed at certain times during the year.

Some religious traditions suggest a memorial service be held on specific dates.

Examples from some religious traditions are to perform a memorial at forty days after the person dies, three months after the person dies, six months after the person dies, one year after the person dies, and three years after the person dies.

A ritual in memory of a person or animal may be performed every year on his or her birthday, or every year on the date of his or her death.

People may perform a ritual on holidays to remember the person who has died.

Rituals in memory and in honor of a person can be performed anytime. It is up to the people performing the ritual, and their traditions, to decide when to do it.

Communication Form

☑ I will check what is true for me.

☐ I would like to participate in a ritual for (name)____________________

☐ The person's or animal's birthday is ____________________

☐ The date of the death of the person or animal is____________________

☐ His or her favorite time of year is____________________

☐ My religion or spiritual path teaches us to have a memorial service, or other ritual at these times: ____________________

____

☐ I think a good date for a ritual may be____________________

☐ I am not interested in planning a ritual, but I would like to go to one for (name)____________________

☐ I do not want to go to a ritual.

☐ I do not want to participate in a ritual now, but I may want to in the future.

☐ I may want to have a ritual on this date:____________________

☐ I have something to say or questions to ask:____________________

____

____

CHAPTER 12: Continuing a Relationship

What does "continuing a relationship" mean?

Relationships are how people are connected to one another. Relationships are usually between people in a family, or between friends, or between people who work or play together, or otherwise between people in their lives.

In this chapter, "continuing a relationship" refers to having a connection with someone, even after the person dies.

See Chapter 18 - Quote 3

Can people continue a relationship with someone who has died?

Yes, it is possible to continue a relationship with someone who has died, especially if there is a strong feeling of love. Or if there is another strong connection, as in the case of "close" people.

What does it mean to be "close" to a person or animal?

Being "close" to a person or animal refers to a type of relationship. A "close relationship" often exists between people who live together, work together, or between people who see each other on a regular basis.

Close relationships may exist between animals and people.

Close relationships may exist between family members, like parents, brothers, sisters, step-brothers and step-sisters, grandparents, aunts, uncles, and cousins.

Close relationships may exist between teachers and students, and special support people like therapists or counselors, doctors, co-workers, neighbors, friends, or others.

Being "close" does not necessarily mean physically close, like standing close to someone.

People who are "close" to a person or an animal usually rely on the person or animal in an emotional, mental, spiritual, and/or physical way. "Close" people have an invisible connection between them.

The invisible connection often consists of friendship, love, and/or caring for each other.

People may be close to one or more than one person or animal.

Communication Form

☑ I will check what is true for me.

☐ I am close to a person, or more than one person.

☐ The people I am close to are (names) ______________________________

____

____

☐ I am close to an animal, or more than one animal.

☐ The animal(s) I am close to are (names) ___________________________

____

____

☐ I do not know if I am close to someone.

☐ I have something to say or questions to ask: _______________________

____

____

"Were you close to him (or her)?"

After a person dies, people sometimes ask **"Were you close to him?"** or **"Were you close to her?"**

They ask this question because it is commonly understood that if the living person was "close" to the one who died, then the living person may have strong reactions and feel various emotions.

Usually people ask this question because they care about the living person. They wonder how he or she is reacting to the death. They may want to say or do something comforting. They may want to try to help.

Communication Form

☑ I will check what is true for me.

☐ I am close to people and/or animals in my life. They are (name) ________

____

☐ Someone whom I am close to may be dying. His or her name is ________

____

☐ Someone whom I am close to has already died. His or her name is ______

____

☐ No one, whom I am close to, has ever died.

☐ I don't understand what it means to be "close" to someone.

☐ I have something to say or questions to ask: ________________________

____

How can people have a relationship with someone who has died?

Having a relationship with someone who has died means that we can still be connected with the person after he or she has died. Here are some ways that people may choose to be connected to the person who has died.

Some people think about the person who has died. They may save a certain time of the day, or the week, to sit in a quiet place, just to think about the person.

Some people feel that they want to help the soul of the person who has died. They do this by praying for the soul of the person. This is what is meant in this book in Chapters 8 and 11, about taking care of the souls of those who have died. The people who are still alive may choose to pray that the person's soul is in a place of peace and love.

After a person has been dead for many months or years, some people may choose to pray to the soul of the person who died, asking for help with things they are dealing with or thinking about.

The ideas in Chapters 8 and 11 are about taking care of the souls of those who have died.

CHAPTER 13: People's Reactions after Someone Dies

How do people react when they learn that a person they know has died?

Most people have some reactions after someone they care about dies.

Some people get busy right away. They may call other family members and friends to tell them that the person has died. Some people have to make arrangements to take care of the body. Some people have to plan the funeral.

Some people do not have anything to do. They may sit quietly or want to be by themselves. Some people may want to be near others.

Some people have emotional reactions, like sadness or anger or another emotion.

If the person or animal had been in a lot of pain before dying, people may be relieved that the person or animal has died and is not in pain anymore.

Some people might not feel anything.

If it was a sudden or an unexpected death, usually people are shocked—they did not expect it to happen. Some people become confused and don't understand what has happened.

Many people have questions about how or when the death happened.

If people were not "close" to the person who died, they may not feel strong emotional reactions. But they still may have questions about how or when the death happened.

This chapter is about people's reactions after a person or an animal dies.

Communication Form

☑ I will check what is true for me.

- ☐ Someone I know has died. I wonder how other people are reacting to the death of (name) ______________________________
- ☐ An animal I know has died. I wonder how other people are reacting to the death of (name) ______________________________
- ☐ I have some reactions to the death of this person or this animal.
- ☐ I will underline or highlight the sentences on the previous page that describe my reactions to the death of the person or animal.
- ☐ I have other reactions. At this time, my reactions are: ______________

  ____
- ☐ I have something to say or questions to ask: ______________________

  ____

  ____

Will things change after someone dies?

After someone dies, there may be changes in my typical daily routine. There may be big changes. There may be small changes. Maybe there will be no changes. A death will affect families and friends differently.

It is a good idea to find out if there are going to be changes in my life. It is a good idea to have someone describe the changes by writing or typing them out, so I can read what we will think will happen each day.

The information can be written on my checklist or schedule for the day, or on a calendar. The written information may include the names of the people I will be with, the things I will do, and the places I will go.

This is how I will know ahead of time, as much as possible, which things will be different and which things will stay the same. This is how I will know what is going to happen.

If we are not sure what is going to happen, then this also could be written on my checklist or schedule for the day. My parent or helper may write at the spot on the list or schedule:

"When we can, we will find out what will happen. Then we will write down what we will do." And then he or she can leave a blank on my schedule to be filled in later.

If something that has been already written down has to change, then we can cross it out and write down the change.

Changes from the typical routine may be easier to handle when I can predict which things will be different and which things will stay the same.

Communication Form

☑ I will check what is true for me.

☐ I want to find out if and when there will be changes in my normal daily routine. I would like to see a list or read a description of what to expect.

☐ I want to find out which things will be different from usual, and which things will stay the same.

☐ There may be new people in my life. They are: ____________________

____

☐ There may be new things to do. They are: ____________________

____

____

☐ These things will probably be different from before: ______________

____

____

☐ These things will probably stay the same as before: ______________

____

____

☐ I have something to say or questions to ask: ____________________

____

____

How do living people react to a death, later on?

In the days, weeks, months, and years following a death people may think about the person or animal who has died.

Different people have different reactions after someone has died. A living person's reactions after someone has died is called "grieving."

The process of grieving can last many days, weeks, months, or years.

While grieving, people may think a lot about the person or animal who has died. They may want to talk about the person or animal who has died. Sometimes people do not want to think about or talk about the person or the animal who has died.

Grieving is a natural reaction after a person or an animal close to us has died.

Grieving is a natural reaction after someone has lost someone or something.

Everybody grieves, sometimes.

What is grieving?

A living person's reaction after someone has died is called "grieving."

Most people grieve after someone or an animal close to them has died. While grieving, people may experience reactions. Some reactions are emotions.

Reactions while grieving are different from one person to another. A common reaction is to feel emotions. Emotions may feel very big and intense inside the person, or emotions may feel small and gentle inside the person.

The intensity of the feelings inside the person may change from minute to minute, and from one day to the next.

Does everyone grieve in the same way after someone dies?

No. After someone dies, every person grieves in his or her own way.

A person may feel different emotions, or feel nothing at all. A person may feel a one way at first, and then feel differently later.

It is natural for emotions to change from day to day, even mintue to minute.

The next several pages describe many of the ways people grieve after someone has died.

It is natural for different people to grieve in different ways after someone has died.

Communication Form

☑ I will check what is true for me.

☐ I think that I may be grieving for a person or an animal who has died.

☐ I do not know if I am grieving.

☐ I need more information about grieving.

☐ I have something to say or questions to ask: ____________________

____

____

What are the most frequent reactions while grieving?

Grieving is not the same for every person. However, researchers have recently discovered that the most frequent reactions of people who are grieving are:

Acceptance: People accept and understand that a person or animal has died.

Yearning: People yearn (wish or want very strongly) to see the person or animal again. They yearn for the person or animal who died.

Communication Form

☑ I will check what is true for me.

- ☐ No one close to me has died.
- ☐ Someone close to me has died. It was (name)____________________
- ☐ More than one person or animal close to me have died. Their names are:

____

____

- ☐ I know and understand that__________ has died. I have accepted this.
- ☐ I am yearning for ________________________________
- ☐ I wish I could see ______________________________ again.
- ☐ I think about this person or this animal a lot.
- ☐ I have something to say or questions to ask:____________________

____

What are common reactions that people have while grieving?

Common reactions while grieving are listed here in alphabetical order. This chapter contains more information about each of these reactions:

- Acceptance
- Anger
- Denial
- Difficulty Thinking
- Fear
- Guilt
- Physical Distress
- Regression
- Sadness
- Yearning

Communication Form

☑ I will check what is true for me.

☐ I will underline the reactions on the list (above) that I have, or had in the past.

☐ I will circle the reactions on the list (above) that I have today.

☐ I want to learn about one or more of these reactions: ________________

____

____

☐ I have something to say or questions to ask: ________________

____

Acceptance

Acceptance means that people know and remember that something is true and real.

In the case of someone who has died, acceptance means that people know and understand that the person has really died. They accept it as a fact. Most people come to accept that the person or animal has died.

They may still experience feelings of sadness and yearning, but they know that it is true and real that the person or animal has died.

Communication Form

☑ I will check what is true for me.

- ☐ I know that (name) ______________________ has died.
- ☐ Sometimes I forget that (name) ______________________ has died.
- ☐ I have accepted the fact that he or she has died.
- ☐ I do not want to think about it.
- ☐ I do not want to talk about it.
- ☐ I do want to learn more about the death of ______________(name).
- ☐ I have something to say or questions to ask: ______________________

____

Anger

Some people may react by feeling angry that someone has died. They may feel a little angry. Or they may feel very angry.

They may feel angry with the person who has died, or with another person who is alive. They may feel angry with the doctors or nurses. They may be angry at someone or something else.

"Rage" is a word for a very intense degree of anger. Milder degrees of anger are "frustration" and "impatience."

Some people may not feel anger at all.

Communication Form

☑ I will check what is true for me.

- ☐ Sometimes I feel angry about (name) ______________________ dying.
- ☐ I feel angry now.
- ☐ I am angry at the person who died.
- ☐ I am angry with other people. The people I am angry with are: (names)__

  ____
- ☐ I feel other degrees of anger about the person dying. Which ones?
  - ☐ Impatience
  - ☐ Frustration
  - ☐ Rage
  - ☐ Other: ______________________________________
- ☐ I am not angry right now.
- ☐ I feel an emotion now, but it is not anger.

Denial

Denial is when people "deny" that the person or animal has died.

They might not believe that the person has really died. They may not want to think about it.

Denial is a natural response that people sometimes have after someone has died. Often people are in denial from time to time after someone has died.

It is okay to take a break from thinking about the person's death.

Sometimes "denial" helps people get through the day; it gives them a rest from feeling strong emotions all the time.

Communication Form

☑ I will check what is true for me.

- ☐ I have been told that someone I know has died, but I do not believe it.
- ☐ I wonder if he or she has really died.
- ☐ I know he or she has died, but sometimes I forget that he or she has died.
- ☐ I do not want to think about the person or animal who has died.
- ☐ I do not want to talk about the person or animal who has died.
- ☐ I do not want to hear about the person or animal who died.
- ☐ I may not want to talk or hear about it now, but I may want to later.
- ☐ I do not want to talk about the person or animal who died, but I do want to hear about him (her). I want someone else to talk about it.
- ☐ I would like help looking through the **Table of Contents** in this book, to find certain information.
- ☐ I want more information about him or her, or about the death. I want this information: ______________________________

  ____
- ☐ I want more information about how he or she died.
- ☐ I have something to say or questions to ask: ______________________________

  ____

Difficulty Thinking

Some people may react by having difficulty thinking clearly. They may have difficulty concentrating or remembering things.

They may have trouble focusing on what they are reading or difficulty doing their work.

They may have trouble paying attention when someone is talking to them.

They may not understand what people are saying to them.

They may forget to do things.

They may forget when to do something or go somewhere.

They may forget where they are supposed to go.

If they drive, they may have trouble focusing on driving. They may think about other things instead of paying attention to driving carefully.

They may become confused or their thoughts may become mixed up.

Difficulty with thinking, concentrating, paying attention, understanding, and remembering things, are common reactions while grieving.

Communication Form

☑ I will check what is true for me.

☐ Sometimes I have difficulty thinking clearly. Sometimes I:

- ☐ have trouble concentrating on what I am doing.
- ☐ don't understand what I am reading.
- ☐ don't understand what someone is saying.
- ☐ can't focus on my work.
- ☐ forget to do things.
- ☐ forget where I am going.
- ☐ think about other things while I am driving.
- ☐ get confused.
- ☐ can't make a decision.

☐ I am having difficulty thinking clearly now.

☐ I don't know if have difficulty with thinking, remembering, concentrating, and other reactions described on the previous page.

☐ I will highlight or underline the words on the previous page that sometimes describe me.

☐ I do not have difficulty with any of these things.

☐ I have noticed that other people in my life have trouble thinking clearly and remembering things.

☐ I have something to say or questions to ask: ______________________

____

Fear

Some people may react by feeling afraid. They may be afraid that something bad might happen to them, or to someone else. They may worry about what has happened and what is going to happen. Or they may feel afraid of other things.

A very intense degree of fear is "terror." Milder degrees of fear are "anxiety" and "nervousness."

Some people may not feel fear at all.

Communication Form

☑ I will check what is true for me.

- ☐ The death of (name)_______________ makes me feel afraid.
- ☐ I feel afraid, now.
- ☐ I am afraid that something bad will happen. I am afraid that: __________

  ____
- ☐ I have been afraid before, but I am not afraid right now.
- ☐ I am worried about something. I am worried that: ________________

  ____
- ☐ I feel other degrees of fear. Which ones?
  - ☐ Worry
  - ☐ Nervousness
  - ☐ Terror
  - ☐ Other: ______________________________
- ☐ I have something to say or questions to ask: ____________________

Guilt

Sometimes people may react by feeling guilty.

When people feel guilty about someone having died, it may mean that they think that it is their fault that he or she died. They may think that if they had done something differently, then the person would not have died. They may feel guilty for how they acted with the person, what they said to the person, or how they felt about the person when he or she was alive.

Or, they may feel guilty that they are still alive, but the other person is not.

Some people may not feel guilty at all.

Communication Form

☑ I will check what is true for me.

☐ I wonder why (name)________________________________ died.

☐ Sometimes I think that it may be my fault that ______________ died.

☐ I think it is my fault because ______________________________

____

☐ Sometimes I think that it may be someone else's fault that he or she died. Maybe it is (name) ______________________________'s fault.

☐ I know that it is no one's fault. Dying is a natural part of life.

☐ I feel guilty for doing or saying certain things when he or she was alive. I feel guilty about____

____

☐ I have something to say or questions to ask:____________________

____

Physical Distress

Some people may have physical reactions in their bodies while they are grieving. For example, they may get stomachaches or headaches. They may get sick. This is called physical distress.

Some people may have accidents. They may move too quickly and not think about where they are going or what they are doing. They may bump into things, or fall or trip when they are walking.

They may become restless or hyperactive.

They may have other physical reactions, like having a cold, a skin rash, difficulty falling asleep, or waking up in the middle of the night and not being able to go back to sleep. Some people may be tired all the time.

Some people may not experience any physical distress.

Communication Form

☑ I will check what is true for me.

☐ I have been sick lately, while in the grieving process.

☐ I have had more accidents than usual, while in the grieving process.

☐ I am experiencing physical distress, now. The illness, accident, or other physical distress I feel now is ______________________________

____

☐ I do not have any physical distress lately.

☐ Other people in my life are experiencing physical distress (illness or accidents). The people are:______________________________

____

☐ I have something to say or questions to ask: ____________________

Regression

Some people may react by regressing when they are grieving.

They may need help with some things that they had already learned to do by themselves. They might have forgotten how to do something that they used to do easily.

Many people do not regress.

Communication Form

☑ I will check what is true for me.

☐ I wonder if I am reacting to someone's death by regressing. I want to find out. I can ask my parent, other family member, therapist, teacher, or friend if I am not sure.

☐ Since the person died, some things are more difficult for me to do. The difficult things to do are ______________________________

____

☐ I want help with ______________________________

____

☐ I need help with______________________________

____

☐ I have something to say or questions to ask: ____________________

____

Sadness

People may react to a death by feeling sad. Some people feel just a little sadness. Some people may feel a deep and intense sadness.

People usually feel sad if the person who died was close to them.

Sometimes a person may feel sad for a long time. A person may feel sad on some days, but not on other days. A person may feel sad at one time during the day, but not at other times during the same day.

Some people may not feel sad, especially if they were not close to the person or animal who died.

See Chapter 18 – Quote 4

Communication Form

☑ I will check what is true for me.

- ☐ I feel sad right now.
- ☐ I have felt sad about (name) ________________ 's death, but not now.
- ☐ My sadness is *(was)* small and gentle.
- ☐ My sadness is *(was)* big and intense.
- ☐ Sometimes the sadness is small, and other times it is big and intense.
- ☐ I do not feel sad about (name) ________________ 's death, at this time.
- ☐ I have something to say or questions to ask: ________________________

____

Yearning

Many people react by missing the person who died.

People may have a very strong desire to see the person alive again. They may think a lot about wanting to see the person again. They want to talk with the person. They may want to hug or hold the person. They may think about the person many times every day.

If it is a very strong desire to see the person again, it is called "yearning." It may be felt as a combination of sadness and a very intense wanting to be with the person again. It also may feel good to spend time thinking about the person and yearning to see him or her.

It is natural for people to yearn for a deceased person or animal who was close to them.

Communication Form

☑ I will check what is true for me.

- ☐ I miss (name) ______________________
- ☐ I wish I could see ______________________ alive, again.
- ☐ I wish I could talk with him or her.
- ☐ I wish we could be together again.
- ☐ I have a yearning to see the person.
- ☐ I do not miss him or her at this time.
- ☐ I have something to say or questions to ask: ______________________

____

What should someone do when a "close person" has died?

First, the person should remember that grieving is natural. In fact, it is healthy to grieve when someone has died.

It can be helpful for the person who is grieving to try to observe and identify his or her reactions. Reactions include thoughts, ideas, desires, questions, feelings, emotions, and behavior.

Reading this book and using the **Communication Forms** may help the person identify his or her reactions. Show the **Communication Forms** to a family member, teacher, trusted friend, therapist, or other support person. These trusted people will read what was marked on the forms and try to understand what is being communicated.

They may ask questions to get more information, so they may understand better. They may have ideas that may help.

Even if the person wants to be alone, it is a good idea to take time before or after being alone, to communicate personal thoughts, wants, needs, ideas, and feelings.

What if I want to be alone?

A person may want to be alone. It is natural and okay to be alone at times.

Even if a person wants to be alone, it is a good idea to communicate with family members and other trusted people about what he or she is thinking or feeling. The **Communication Forms** in this book may help make it easier to communicate with other people.

Sometimes a person may experience the reactions of grief strongly, with a lot of intensity. If a person feels emotions intensely, it is important to communicate with family members, trusted friends, or therapists. Family members, trusted friends, and therapists can help keep the person safe.

Communication Form

☑ I will check what is true for me.

- ☐ I want to be alone sometimes.
- ☐ I don't want to talk right now, but I will try to communicate by writing on the **Communication Forms.**
- ☐ I want to talk with someone, now.
- ☐ I want to talk to (name) ______________________________
- ☐ I want to write, instead of talking.
- ☐ I want a person to write to me, instead of talking to me.
- ☐ I want the person to write to me, *and* talk to me.
- ☐ I am feeling emotions now. I will go to the lists of different words for emotions in Chapter 14. I will try to circle the words on the lists that best describe what I am feeling.
- ☐ I want to know what ____________________________ means.
- ☐ I want or need something.
- ☐ I want or need ______________________________ .
- ☐ I do not know what I am feeling.
- ☐ Help me find a good safe place where I can go sometimes to be alone.
- ☐ I have something to say or questions to ask: __________________

  ____

What does "being safe" mean?

"Being safe" means that a person treats himself or herself in a kind and healthy manner. Being safe means that a person is not in danger and does not have a high risk of injury in the moment. Being safe means that a person is not going to hurt himself or herself.

If a person needs help staying safe, he or she must ask someone for help. This is an intelligent and wise thing to do.

It is intelligent and necessary to communicate with a trusted person all details of any unsafe thoughts, ideas, plans, or actions.

Communication Form

☑ I will check what is true for me.

- ☐ I try to be safe most of the time.
- ☐ I have thought of doing something that may be harmful or be dangerous. This is what I thought about doing, and when I thought about it: ______

  ____

  ____
- ☐ I have tried to do something harmful or dangerous. These are the details, including the approximate date and time: ______________

  ____

  ____
- ☐ I want to be safe.
- ☐ I am not sure if I am safe by myself. I think I may need help staying safe.
- ☐ I have something to say or questions to ask: ______________

How long will the grieving process last?

The grieving process happens over a period of time, different for every person.

It may last for days, weeks, months, or years. It may start right after someone dies. Some people may not grieve until weeks or months or even years after someone dies.

People often experience grieving reactions for many years, especially sadness and yearning at special occasions like holidays and birthdays. Sometime a grieving reaction may suddenly occur. People may experience grieving reactions in certain locations, or when they hear certain music, songs, or other sounds that remind them of the person who died. They may experience grieving reactions when they smell certain scents or odors that may remind them of the person who died.

Some people may not grieve at all.

Communication Form

☑ I will check what is true for me.

☐ I think I am in the grieving process. I think I started grieving on (approximate date): ______________________________

☐ I don't know if I am in a grieving process.

☐ Sometimes I feel sad about a person or animal who has died.

☐ Sometimes I yearn to see the person or animal who has died. I wish I could see him or her again.

☐ Sometimes I think about the person or animal who died, but sometimes I don't think about him or her at all.

☐ I have something to say or questions to ask: ____________________

Why do people say that grieving "comes in waves"?

Some people compare the feelings and emotions of the grieving process to waves in the ocean.

They say that sometimes the "waves of grief" are mild and gentle. It can be compared to person floating up and down gently in the waves of the ocean.

Other times the ocean waves might be so big and loud that they knock the person down. These big waves are compared to very strong, intense feelings and emotions that may feel overwhelming. An example of an overwhelming emotion is yearning to see the person who has died and feeling so sad that a person cries and cries.

After a time, the ocean waves subside, and the ocean becomes calm again. The calmness of the ocean is compared to the calmness people may experience between the waves of strong emotions.

The calmness is comfortable. The calmness may last for minutes, hours, days, weeks, or months.

This is how grieving comes in "waves."

Communication Form

☑ I will check what is true for me.

- ☐ Sometimes I think about the person or animal who died.
- ☐ The feelings of grief seem to come and go, and come and go again.
- ☐ Sometimes I feel comfortable. The emotions are mild and gentle. It can be compared to the gentle feeling of floating softly in the waves in the ocean.
- ☐ Sometimes I feel overwhelmed. It can be compared to being knocked down by big ocean waves. It may be difficult to think about anything else.
- ☐ "Waves" do not describe my grieving process.
- ☐ I am not grieving.
- ☐ I have something to say or questions to ask: ______________________

  ____

Why do people say that grieving is "like a roller coaster"?

Some people compare the feelings and emotions of the grieving process to a roller coaster. It can be compared to a person riding a roller coaster that goes up and down.

Sometimes the person feels good and "up," like being on the top of a roller coaster hill. Life is good. Most things are going okay.

And then, all of a sudden, the person may feel very sad … and sink "down," like the fast downward ride of a roller coaster. The downward emotional ride may sometimes feel out of control.

The feelings of grief may come and go, quickly, like riding up and down, again and again, on a roller coaster.

Communication Form

☑ I will check what is true for me.

- ☐ Sometimes I think about the person or animal who died.
- ☐ My feelings of grief seem to come and go, and come and go again.
- ☐ Sometimes life feels good, okay, or "up," like being at the top on a roller coaster ride.
- ☐ Sometimes I feel "down," like being on a roller coaster and suddenly, quickly, heading straight down.
- ☐ A "roller coaster" does not describe my grieving process.
- ☐ I am not grieving.
- ☐ I have something to say or questions to ask: ____________________

____

What are some activities that may help people through their grieving?

Being creative may help people while they are grieving.

Being physically active may help people while they are grieving.

They may engage in drawing, cartooning, painting, writing, drumming, inventing games, dancing, playing a musical instrument, singing, photography, making collages, or something else.

They may participate in gardening, going for walks, hiking, bicycling, running, swimming, roller-skating, shooting baskets, martial arts, exercise and weight machines, kicking a ball, sports, and other physical activities.

These types of active and creative behaviors are healthy ways to move through the grieving process.

See Chapter 18 - Quote 5

Communication Form

☑ I will check what is true for me.

☐ I like to be creative or active. I can highlight or underline the ideas in the paragraph above that I would like to do.

☐ I have other ideas of something creative or active to do. My ideas are____

____

☐ I have something to say or questions to ask: ____________________

____

What if I am angry at the person or animal who has died?

Sometimes people who are still alive feel angry when person or animal close to them has died.

It is natural to feel angry sometimes.

It is a good idea to try to put the angry feelings into words by talking or by writing. It may be helpful to write down the angry thoughts with pen and paper, or on a computer, and give it to a family member, close friend, or a therapist to read.

Communicating about angry thoughts is an intelligent and safe thing to do.

Being active and/or creative on a regular basis may help the anger resolve into a peaceful feeling.

It is good to allow time to communicate, to engage in creative activities, and to participate in physical activity on the regular daily schedule.

Times for these things can be written into the daily schedule.

Communication Form

☑ I will check what is true for me.

- ☐ Sometimes I feel angry about (name) ________________________ dying.
- ☐ I am angry about ____
- ☐ I would like to talk about it with someone.
- ☐ I don't want to talk, but I will write or type the answers to questions.
- ☐ I do not want to communicate about it, now.
- ☐ I would like to communicate about it, later.
- ☐ My choice for a creative activity is ______________________________
- ☐ My choice for physical activity is ________________________________
- ☐ Other choices I like for creative and physical activity are ____________

  ____
- ☐ I have something to say or questions to ask: ________________________

  ____

What about school, work, and other responsibilities and activities?

It is important to remember that after someone dies, daily life continues for those of us who are still alive. This means that even though we may be grieving, we still have lives to live.

If a person is a student, he or she usually will go back to school. If a person has a job, he or she usually will continue to work.

There may be rare exceptions, depending on the situation. For example, a person may have to go to a different school, or get a different job.

It is healthy and intelligent to try to do the things that one needs to do at school and at work. It is helpful for people to keep busy.

It is also okay to take time to rest. Sometimes it is helpful to get more rest than usual.

It is good to continue with a regular daily routine.

Communication Form

☑ I will check what is true for me.

- ☐ I wonder if I will continue to attend the same school.
- ☐ I wonder if I will continue to work at the same job.
- ☐ I want to stay on my regular daily routine.
- ☐ I wonder what my regular daily routine is.
- ☐ I don't have a regular daily routine.
- ☐ I would like help figuring out a daily routine.
- ☐ I would like help figuring out a weekly routine.
- ☐ There are things I like to do. I want to make sure that I keep doing them when possible. They are: ______________________________

  ____

  ____
- ☐ I would like to do more things.
- ☐ I need more time to rest.
- ☐ I don't know what I need or want, now.
- ☐ I have something to say or questions to ask: ______________________________

  ____

Do feelings stay the same or do they change?

Feelings change as life goes on.

Feelings are a part of life.

Change is a part of life.

For example, a person who feels sad will not feel sad forever. Sometimes the sad feelings change to happiness. It is also okay to laugh when grieving.

A person who feels angry does not have to be angry forever. It is natural for angry feelings to subside and to begin to feel more peaceful.

A person may sometimes feel happy or peaceful and then feel sad, or angry, and then peaceful or happy again.

Feelings may change from day to day. Feelings will change as a person lives and grows. This is the natural process of living.

If feelings change too quickly, or if they go up and down rapidly from one extreme to another, or if people are confused by their feelings, then it is important to tell a trusted person, like a family member or therapist.

Communication Form

☑ I will check what is true for me.

- ☐ My feelings change. I may write a list of feelings that I have had, or I can go to Chapter 13 and 14 to find the words that describe how I feel. The words that describe how I feel are: ______________________________

  ____

  ____

  ____

- ☐ I think my feelings change too much. Sometimes it is confusing.
- ☐ I am okay about my feelings. I understand that they may change.
- ☐ I have a person whom I trust to talk with about my feelings. His or her name is ______________________________________ .
- ☐ Most of the time, I do not know how I feel.
- ☐ I am not interested in the topic of feelings.
- ☐ I have something to say or questions to ask: ____________________

  ____

Do people always feel strong emotions after someone has died?

No, not always. There may be some people who do not feel strong emotions after someone has died. If the person or animal who died was not close to them, then they might not feel strong emotions about the death.

This is okay.

There may be some people who typically do not experience strong emotions in their regular day-to-day lives. These people may not experience the grieving process with strong feelings and emotions. Their reactions to the death of a person or an animal may be different from other people's reactions.

Some people feel strong emotions and some people do not feel strong emotions.

A person may feel emotions on the inside, but not express the emotions on the outside.

Feeling emotions is different from **expressing emotions.**

Communication Form

☑ I will check what is true for me.

☐ A person or animal in my life has died. I feel strong emotions about his or her death. The emotions I feel are ______________________________

____

____

☐ I feel emotions about his or her death, but they are gentle emotions—not too intense or strong. I feel ______________________________

____

____

☐ Sometimes my emotions are mild and sometimes they are intense.

☐ I do not feel any emotions about the death of this person or animal.

☐ I feel emotions inside myself, but I do not want to talk about them.

☐ I usually do not express my emotions.

☐ I am not sure what emotions I feel about the death.

☐ I have something to say or questions to ask: ______________________

____

What is the difference between feeling emotions and expressing emotions?

Feeling emotions is different from **expressing** emotions.

Feeling emotions is what a person experiences inside himself or herself. The names of general categories of emotions are sadness, happiness, anger, and fear. Other words to describe emotions are listed in Chapter 14.

Feeling emotions can sometimes be compared to being inside a box. It can feel like the emotions are inside a box—inside the body.

When a person feels emotions on the inside, other people may not know what the person is feeling. Other people cannot easily see inside the "box."

Expressing emotions is when a person **shows on the outside of his or her body,** how he or she feels inside his or her body. Expressing emotions can be compared to opening the box and letting the emotions come out. Common ways of expressing emotions are smiling, laughing, frowning, and crying.

Other good ways of expressing emotions are through talking or writing. When people talk or write, they describe in words what they are feeling.

Drawing, playing music, dancing, and other art forms are be more ways of expressing emotions.

Feeling emotions happens on the **inside** of the person.

Expressing emotions can be seen on the **outside** of the person.

Communication Form

☑ I will check what is true for me.

- ☐ I usually know when I feel emotions.
- ☐ I usually do not know when I feel emotions.
- ☐ I feel emotions inside myself, but usually do not express them to others.
- ☐ Sometimes I express how I feel. Sometimes I:
  - ☐ Talk about the emotions I feel.
  - ☐ Write about the emotions I feel.
  - ☐ Cry when I am with someone.
  - ☐ Smile or laugh when I am with someone.
  - ☐ Yell when I am with someone.
  - ☐ Draw or paint pictures to express the emotions I feel.
  - ☐ Sing to express the emotions I feel.
  - ☐ Make music (with an instrument) to express the emotions I feel.
  - ☐ Play music (CDs) to express the emotions I feel.
  - ☐ Dance to express the emotions I feel.
  - ☐ Use another art form to express the emotions I feel. I do this: ______

    ____
- ☐ Sometimes people ask me, **"How do you feel?"**
- ☐ I don't know how to answer the question, **"How do you feel?"**
- ☐ The list above has given me some ideas. I would like to try one or more of those ways of expressing emotions. I would like to try ______________
- ☐ I have something to say or questions to ask: ______________________

  ____

The Question: "How do you feel?"

This is an often-asked question by friends, family members, teachers, therapists, and others.

When people ask, "**How do you feel?**" it means that they cannot see from the outside of the person how he or she feels on the inside.

Or they may try to guess how the person feels, but they may not be right. This is why they ask. They ask because they need or want more information.

Usually people ask, "**How do you feel?**" because they care about the person and they want to understand what the person feels inside.

Trying to answer this question helps other people understand what a person is feeling inside.

See Chapter 18 - Quote 6

Communication Form

☑ I will check what is true for me.

- ☐ Sometimes people ask me "**How do you feel?**"
- ☐ I wonder why (name) ______________ asks me "**How do you feel?**"
- ☐ I usually try to answer the question by naming the emotion(s) that I feel.
- ☐ I usually avoid answering the question. I usually do not like to answer.
- ☐ I usually know how I feel, but I do not know how to say it.
- ☐ I usually know how I feel, but I cannot find the right words.
- ☐ I would like to learn how to express my feelings accurately.
- ☐ I don't want to talk about my feelings.
- ☐ I don't want to tell someone else my feelings.
- ☐ I don't want to talk about my feelings, but I would like to write or type about them.
- ☐ Most of the time I do not know how I feel.
- ☐ I would like to ask other people this question. I want to ask someone the question "**How do you feel?**" I want to ask the following people this question: ____

  ____

  ____
- ☐ I have another question or something to say: ______________________

  ____

Why do some people not cry after someone dies?

Each person alive has a unique relationship with the person or animal who has died. Each person may react differently when a person or animal dies.

In the case of someone's death who was not "close," it is natural to not cry. Or, a person may cry, even if they did not know the person well.

In other cases, people may simply accept the fact that someone has died. They may not cry.

Sometimes small tears seep slowly out of people's eyes, and the tears are so small that other people cannot see the tears. Other people don't know that the people are crying because their tears are not noticed.

Some people cry when they are alone, and no one sees them crying.

People may still care about or love the person or animal who died, even if they do not react by crying.

Communication Form

☑ I will check what is true for me.

- ☐ I cared about the person or animal who died.
- ☐ I loved the person or animal who died.
- ☐ I was close to him (or her).
- ☐ I was not close to him (or her).
- ☐ Sometimes I still think about him (or her).
- ☐ I feel sad about his (or her) death.
- ☐ I have cried about the death, but I am not crying now.
- ☐ I cried when I was alone.
- ☐ I cried when I was near other people, but my maybe tears were so small, no one could see that I was crying. They may think that I didn't cry.
- ☐ I miss the person or animal who died. I wish I could see him or her again, alive.
- ☐ I do not think about him (or her) very much.
- ☐ I have something to say or questions to ask: ______________________________

____

What does "apathy" or "apathetic" mean?

Apathy means "lack of emotions or interest."

When people are apathetic they are not interested in life. They do not want to do anything. They do not feel anything. Often people who are apathetic may feel very tired.

Sometimes people are apathetic when they are in the grieving process.

Sometimes people are apathetic when they are depressed.

If a person is apathetic for more than a few weeks, it is a good idea to follow the advice of family members, trusted friends, or a therapist.

Following good advice may help the person begin to be interested in things again. Interest in doing things, reading about things, or otherwise participating in life, may begin to replace the apathy.

Communication Form

☑ I will check what is true for me.

- ☐ I do not want to do anything.
- ☐ I do not care about the things I used to enjoy.
- ☐ I am tired most of the time.
- ☐ Maybe I am depressed.
- ☐ I have lots of energy.
- ☐ I feel good.
- ☐ I want to do certain things. They are: ______________________
- ☐ I have something to say or questions to ask: ______________________

What does "acceptance" mean?

"Acceptance" means that people know and remember that something is true.

In the case of someone who has died, acceptance means that people know and understand that the person has really died. They accept it as a fact. They may feel sad or angry or have other feelings, but they know it is true and real that the person or animal has died.

Fully accepting that someone has died may take a long time.

Communication Form

☑ I will check what is true for me.

- ☐ I know that (name) ______________________ has died.
- ☐ It is true that (name) ______________________ has died.
- ☐ I am not sure that she (or he) has really died.
- ☐ It's hard to remember that she (or he) has died.
- ☐ Sometimes I don't believe that (name) ________________ died.
- ☐ Sometimes I pretend that (name) ________________ hasn't died.
- ☐ I have accepted that (name) ______________________ has died.
- ☐ I have something to say or questions to ask: ________________

  ____

What does it mean to make "adjustments"?

To make "adjustments" means to revise or to change how something is done or how things happen.

It means to "adjust" some things.

For example, if the person who died was a teacher, then one adjustment that the school would make would be to hire a new teacher.

Another adjustment would be that the students would have to get used to hearing the new teacher's voice and how the new teacher gives directions.

Another adjustment might be that a student would have to ask for help if he or she does not understand the new teacher.

Adjustments often include asking for help, even if the person didn't usually need help before.

When someone dies, adjustments usually have to be made by the people who are still alive.

Communication Form

☑ I will check what is true for me.

- ☐ A family member of mine has died.
- ☐ A close friend of mine has died.
- ☐ A person who was in my life at school has died.
- ☐ Someone at work has died.
- ☐ A person whom I know from my community has died.
- ☐ A person who was in my life has died.
- ☐ I will have to make some adjustments in my life now.
- ☐ I think some of the adjustments I will have to make are: ____________

  ____

  ____

- ☐ I am not sure what the adjustments will be.
- ☐ I want more information about adjustments that I will have to make.
- ☐ I can get help from (name)____________to plan the adjustments in my life, now.
- ☐ Some of the adjustments will be the following things: ____________

  ____

  ____

- ☐ I have something to say or questions to ask:____________________

CHAPTER 14: More Names for Emotions

Why learn the names of different emotions?

"**How are you feeling?**" is a question that is often asked of people when changes have occurred in their lives. The death of a person or animal is considered to be a big change.

Sometimes people answer "**I don't know.**" When people answer "**I don't know,**" it might be because they do not know the name, or the word that describes how they feel.

This chapter introduces words—the names—for general categories of emotional responses, with other words that fall under the general categories.

Communication Form

☑ I will check what is true for me.

- ☐ Sometimes people ask me "**How are you feeling?**"
- ☐ I rarely am asked "**How are you feeling?**"
- ☐ I really don't understand what "**How are you feeling?**" means.
- ☐ I usually answer by saying how I feel.
- ☐ I usually do not know how to answer this question.
- ☐ I usually don't know how I feel. I don't know what to answer.
- ☐ I usually know how I feel, but I don't answer.
- ☐ Usually I answer the question by saying "**I don't know.**"
- ☐ Sometimes it's difficult to explain in words how I feel.
- ☐ I don't know why other people want to know how I feel.
- ☐ Other people think they know how I feel, but they really do not.

What are the names of general categories of emotions?

A few general categories for emotions are listed below.

- Happiness
- Fear
- Anger
- Sadness
- Surprise
- Interest

Communication Form

☑ I will check what is true for me.

☐ Sometimes I feel happy. An example of a time I felt happy is: ________

____

☐ Sometimes I feel afraid. An example of a time when I felt afraid is: _____

____

☐ Sometimes I feel angry. An example of a time when I felt angry is:______

____

☐ Sometimes I feel sad. An example of a time when I felt sad is: ________

____

☐ Sometimes I feel surprised. An example of a time when I felt surprised is:

____

☐ Sometimes I feel interested in something or someone. An example of a time I felt interested is: ________________________________

☐ I feel emotions, but the words on the list do not express how I have felt.

Happiness: What are more words that describe degrees of happiness?

People may feel varying degrees of happiness. Examples of words in the category of happiness are listed below. The words toward the top of the list describe strong feelings of happiness. The words toward the bottom of the list describe mild or gentle feelings of happiness.

- Blissful
- Gleeful
- Joyful
- Elated
- Happy
- Cheerful
- Glad
- Content
- Well
- Satisfied

Communication Form

☑ I will check what is true for me.

☐ I have felt one or more of those emotions sometime in my life. If so, I will underline the ones I have felt.

☐ One of these words describes how I am feeling now. I will circle the word that describes how I am feeling now.

☐ There is no word to describe how I feel when ______________________

☐ I am interested in learning more about one or more of the words on this list. The words I am interested in are: ______________________

☐ I have something to say or questions to ask: ______________________

Fear: What are more words that describe degrees of fear?

People may feel varying degrees of fear. Examples of words in the category of fear are listed below.

The words toward the top of the list describe strong or intense feelings of fear. The words toward the bottom describe mild, gentle, or small feelings of fear.

- Terrified
- Fearful
- Afraid
- Anxious
- Nervous
- Worried
- Shy
- Doubtful

Communication Form

☑ I will check what is true for me.

☐ I have felt one or more of those emotions sometime in my life. If so, I will underline the ones I have felt.

☐ One of these words describes how I am feeling now. I will circle the word that describes how I am feeling now.

☐ There is another word that describes an emotion in the category of fear that I feel. The word is ____ .

☐ There is no word to describe how I feel when ________________________

____

☐ I am interested in learning more about one or more of the words on this list. The words I am interested in are: ____________________________

Anger: What are more words that describe degrees of anger?

People may feel varying degrees of anger. Examples of words considered in the category of anger are listed below.

The words toward the top of the list describe strong or intense feelings of anger. The words toward the bottom describe mild, gentle, or small feelings of anger.

- Enraged
- Hostile
- Angry
- Resentful
- Frustrated
- Irritated
- Impatient

Communication Form

☑ I will check what is true for me.

☐ I have felt one or more of those emotions sometime in my life. If so, I will underline the ones I have felt.

☐ One of these words describes how I am feeling now. I will circle the word that describes how I am feeling now.

☐ There is another word that describes an emotion in the category of anger that I feel. The word is______________________________

☐ There is no word to describe how I feel when____________________

☐ I am interested in learning more about one or more of the words on this list. I am interested in learning about: ________________________

Sadness: What are words that describe degrees of sadness?

People may feel varying degrees of sadness. Examples of words in the category of sadness are listed below. The words toward the top of the list describe strong or intense feelings of sadness. The words toward the bottom describe mild, gentle, or small feelings of sadness.

- Miserable
- Depressed
- Despondent
- Grieved
- Forlorn
- Sorrowful
- Sad
- Unhappy
- Disappointed

Communication Form

☑ I will check what is true for me.

☐ I have felt one or more of those emotions sometime in my life. If so, I will underline the ones I have felt.

☐ One of these words describes how I am feeling now. I will circle the word that describes how I am feeling now.

☐ There is another word that describes an emotion in the category of sadness that I feel. The word is ____________________

☐ There is no word to describe how I feel when ____________________

____

☐ I am interested in learning more about: ____________________

Surprise: What are words that describe degrees of surprise?

People may feel varying degrees of surprise. Examples of words in the category of surprise are listed below.

The words toward the top of the list describe strong or intense feelings of surprise. The words toward the bottom describe mild, gentle, or small feelings of surprise.

- Shocked
- Astonished
- Amazed
- Confused
- Surprised
- Startled

Communication Form

☑ I will check what is true for me.

☐ I have felt one or more of those emotions sometime in my life. If so, I will underline the ones I have felt.

☐ One of these words describes how I am feeling now. I will circle the word that describes how I am feeling now.

☐ There is another word that describes an emotion in the category of surprise that I feel. The word is ______________________________

☐ There is no word to describe how I feel when ______________________

____

☐ I am interested in learning more about one or more of the words on this list. I am interested in the words: ____________________________

Interest: What are words that describe degrees of interest?

People may feel varying degrees of interest.

Examples of words in the category of interest are listed below.

The words toward the top of the list describe strong or intense feelings of interest. The words toward the bottom describe mild, gentle, or small feelings of interest.

- Enthusiastic
- Enthralled
- Absorbed
- Fascinated
- Interested
- Curious

Communication Form

☑ I will check what is true for me.

☐ I have felt one or more of these emotions sometime in my life. If so, I will underline the ones I have felt.

☐ One of these words describes how I am feeling now. I will circle the word that describes how I am feeling now.

☐ There is another word that describes an emotion in the category of interest that I feel. The word is________________________________

☐ There is no word to describe how I feel when______________________

____

☐ I am interested in learning more about one or more of the words on this list. I am interested in the words:______________________________

How can a person learn more about feelings and emotions?

If a person is wants to learn more about feelings and emotions, he or she can read books on the subject, research the Internet, and talk with certain people, such as therapists, teachers, parents, friends, or others.

Dictionaries may help with definitions. Talking with a trusted person may help with understanding the definitions.

One way to study emotions is to make a list of different emotions, and keep a record of when these emotions are felt in daily life.

Writing down thoughts, ideas, and feelings on a regular basis is called **keeping a journal**. Many people keep a journal. Keeping a journal may help a person identify and understand his or her feelings.

Keeping a journal may also help a person more easily express his or her feelings.

Some people may choose to show their parents, therapists, or others some things they have written in their journal. It may help other people better understand him or her.

Communication Form

☑ I will check what is true for me.

☐ I am interested in learning more about feelings and emotions. I am interested in the following:

- ☐ Reading a book or several books on feelings and emotions.
- ☐ Researching on the Internet.
- ☐ Talking (or writing) with a therapist or teacher.
- ☐ Talking (or writing) with a parent or other family member.
- ☐ Talking (or writing) with someone else:________________________
- ☐ Keeping a journal in a book or computer.
- ☐ Other ideas: ____

____

____

____

____

Chapter 15: What Does it Means If Someone Says ...

What does it mean if someone says, "I want to die" or "I want to kill myself" or "Why don't you just kill me?"

Sometimes children, teenagers, and adults become very upset. They may say things quickly and automatically when they are upset. Another word for this is that they say things "impulsively."

Impulsive means to do or say something before thinking carefully and intelligently. Impulsive reactions are more likely to happen when people feel strong emotions.

These statements are extreme examples of what some people may say impulsively when they are very very anxious, upset, or angry:

- **I want to die.**
- **I want to kill myself.**
- **Why don't you just kill me?**
- **I wish I was dead.**

After calming down, the person who said these statements may realize that the words are not really true. The person may not literally mean that they want to die.

Or the statements above may be true for the person. He or she may be very depressed. More information about these statements is included in this chapter.

Communication Form

☑ I will check what is true for me.

- ☐ This information is not relevant to me. I am not interested in this topic.
- ☐ I am interested in this topic.
- ☐ This information may be important to me.
- ☐ This information may be relevant to me.
- ☐ I understand what it means to say something "impulsively."
- ☐ I do not understand what "impulsive" means.
- ☐ I have questions or something to say about this:____________________

____

____

How do these statements become a routine?

Sometimes a person says "**I want to die**" or "**I want to kill myself**" or "**Why don't you just kill me?**" or other similar statements, when he or she is very anxious or feeling strong emotions, like sadness, misery, depression, anger, rage, hostility, or another emotion.

The statements, repeated over and over, may become attached to feeling a strong emotion. So, when the person feels that strong emotion, he or she may automatically repeat the same statement.

If it happens frequently, the statement may become a routine.

Communication Form

☑ I will check what is true for me.

☐ This information is not meaningful to me. I am not interested in this topic.

☐ I am interested in this topic.

☐ I sometimes say routine statements, but I don't remember what they are. I will ask someone I trust to help me remember.

☐ I do say routine statements. I sometimes say these things: ____________

____

____

____

☐ I have questions or something to say: ____________________________

____

____

How can it be helpful to know if I have a routine of saying certain statements?

Routine statements such as "**I want to die**" or "**Why don't you just kill me?**" are usually attached to emotions such as frustration, anger, fear, worry, hostility, depression, or another emotion.

It may be that the person who says these things is very unhappy about something. He or she may want something to stop. He or she may need to get away from something. It probably means that something needs to change in the person's life.

With help, the person can learn to identify what is needed or wanted. He or she can learn to use other words that communicate more accurately what is wanted or needed.

For example, when something is needed or wanted, instead of repeating the routine statemtent about wanting to die, the person tries to remember to begin the statement with these words, followed by accurate information that is true for the person:

- **"I need ...."**
- **"I don't need ...."**
- **"I want ...."**
- **"I don't want ...."**
- **"Help me to ...."**
- **Other:** ______________________________

Using words that accurately communicate what is needed or wanted may help other people understand better.

Other people may be able to help the person make changes for the better when they understand more about the person.

Read more about communication in Chapter 5.

Communication Form

☑ I will check what is true for me.

☐ This information is not meaningful to me. I am not interested in this topic.

☐ I think that I sometimes say a routine statement. Sometimes I say: _____

____

____

☐ The true reason for my routine statement may be that:

- ☐ Something needs to stop. This is what needs to stop:____________

  ____

- ☐ I need or want something. It is:______________________________

  ____

- ☐ I am unhappy about something. I feel unhappy about this: _______

  ____

- ☐ Something else. It is: _________________________________

  ____

☐ I do not know the true reason for my routine phrase.

☐ I want to figure out the true reason for my routine phrase.

☐ I will ask (name) ____________________________ for help with this.

☐ I have something to say or questions to ask: ______________________

____

What does it mean if someone is *depressed*, and says "I want to die" or "I want to kill myself," or if he or she is thinking of ways to die?

If a person says these things, it is important to find out if it is being said impulsively, if it is a routine, or if it is really true that he or she wants to die. If the person truly feels like wanting to die, he or she may be depressed.

Being depressed is serious. It is an illness. The name of this illness is "depression."

People may be depressed if they feel sad all the time—for many days or weeks or months. They may cry often. Or, they may not feel anything, and are tired all the time. They may sleep too much, or they may not be able to sleep at all. They may eat too much or not want to eat at all.

They don't enjoy the things that used to make them happy. They may not enjoy reading or talking about their interests. They may not be able to concentrate or stay focused. They may not want to do anything at all. They may stay in bed for a long time when it is not their usual time to sleep.

If this describes how a person is for many weeks or months, he or she may be depressed.

Sometimes, when a person is depressed day after day for a long time, they may think about not living anymore. They may think of ways to die. The person who is depressed should tell someone else the thoughts about dying.

Other people do not know the person's internal thoughts unless the person tells them. Other people do not know how the person feels inside unless the person tells them.

It is important that the person who is depressed communicate with someone. It is important to get help.

It is important that other people get help for a person who is depressed and thinking about dying.

Communication Form

☑ I will check what is true for me.

- ☐ This information is not relevant to me. I am not interested in this topic.
- ☐ I am interested in this topic.
- ☐ This information may be relevant to me.
- ☐ If I say, "**I want to die,**" I mean it. Sometimes I think about wanting to die even when I don't say it aloud.
- ☐ I have thought about and planned ways to die.
- ☐ I think that I may be depressed. If so, I will highlight or underline the sentences on the previous pages that sometimes describe me.
- ☐ There is a person, or more than one person in my life with whom I may communicate. They may be family members, teachers, therapists, close friends, or others. Her, his, or their names are:____________________

  ____
- ☐ I will contact one or more of these people in person, by phone, or by email. **It is suggested by the author of this book that I show them these pages of this book, as soon as possible.**
- ☐ I do not know how or with whom to communicate about the possibility of depression and thoughts of dying. **It is suggested by the author of this book to show this page to someone I trust. Or, if I do not know anyone to contact, I should contact a doctor, a therapist, a minister or rabbi, the local hospital, or call a local "hotline" and ask to talk with a person about feeling depressed and thinking about dying.**
- ☐ If I communicate with a professional, a therapist, a minister or rabbi, a doctor, or local hotline, it would be helpful to tell the person that I have Asperger's, (or ASD, or autism), and if possible, show the person pages 12-13 titled "**A Close Look at Communication.**"

Why should a person get help if he or she is depressed?

Having the illness called depression is similar to having another illness, like pneumonia, influenza, strep throat, ear infections, or other illnesses.

When people are sick for more than a week, they should get help from a doctor.

Doctors and/or therapists can help people who are sick with depression. There is medication and/or other therapy to help a person who has the illness called depression.

It is wise to get help if a person has questions about depression, or if a person thinks he or she may be depressed.

The first step in getting help is to communicate with someone. Showing someone these pages of this book is an intelligent thing to do.

The author recommends showing these pages to a doctor, therapist, support person, a family member, or another trusted person.

Communication Form

☑ I will check what is true for me.

☐ There is a person, or more than one person, in my life with whom I sometimes communicate. They may be family members, teachers, therapists, close friends, or others. Her, his, or their names are:

____

____

☐ I will circle the names of one or more than one of those people to communicate with, about being depressed.

☐ I will choose the method of communication:

- ☐ Phone
- ☐ Email
- ☐ Talk in person
- ☐ Show her/him/them this page of the book
- ☐ Write a letter and mail it
- ☐ Other:____

____

☐ There is no one in my life with whom I can communicate. If this is true, I should contact a doctor, a therapist, the local hospital, or call a local "hotline" and ask to talk with someone about feeling depressed and thinking about dying. It is important to tell the person that I have Aspergers, (or ASD, or autism), and if possible, show the person pages 12-13 titled **"A Close Look at Communication."**

CHAPTER 16: What People May Learn About Life When Facing Death

What does it mean to "face death"?

People who have "faced death" may have been with someone who is dying, or they have known someone who has died.

Facing death could also mean that they have been very, very sick themselves, but they recovered—they did not die from the illness or injury.

Or they may have been in a serious accident, but they survived—they did not die from the accident.

Or they may be in the process of dying, now.

When people face death, they may think about their lives. They often think about how they have lived, and what they have learned about life.

People who have faced death often think about how they want to live the rest of their days.

See Chapter 18 - Quote 7

Communication Form

☑ I will check what is true for me.

☐ I have known someone who has died. His or her name is______________

☐ I have thought about death.

☐ I have thought about life.

☐ I have thought about how I want to live each day.

☐ I have questions or something to say: ____________________________

____

What are some of the things people may think about when they face death?

When people face death, they may think about their lives.

They may remember events from their childhood, or things that happened when they were older.

Sometimes they think about certain people in their lives—friends, family members, teachers, and others. They may be thankful for certain people, things, and events.

Sometimes they wish they had done certain things differently.

Sometimes people think about the meaning of life. They may think about what happens after they die. Some people think about their beliefs in the afterlife or about God.

When we know someone who is dying, or has died, it may prompt us to think about our lives in these ways.

Some things people may think about are listed below. They are described, one by one, in this chapter.

- Appreciation and Gratitude
- Regret
- Forgiveness
- Self-knowledge
- Acceptance
- Fear
- Courage
- People
- Tolerance
- Respect
- Kindness

- Honesty
- The Combination of Honesty, Respect, and Kindness
- Uncertainty
- Faith
- God
- Fulfillment
- Love
- Truth
- Reality

I will circle the things on the list that interest me. More information on these topics can be found in essays, stories, poetry, movies, DVDs, and other sources in libraries, bookstores, and the Internet. Talking with certain people about these topics may also be helpful.

Appreciation and Gratitude

To appreciate means to cherish and value something. Gratitude means thankfulness. People may appreciate and be grateful for things, ideas, people, opportunities, events, experiences, and life itself.

Many people realize that it is important to be grateful for the little things that happen each day.

When facing death, many people become grateful for things that they usually don't notice, like clean air to breathe, or a warm house when it is cold outside, or good food to eat, or a functional computer, or a family member who cares for them. They begin to appreciate what they have experienced in life.

They may choose to say "thank you" to certain people who are important to them. They may choose to say "thank you" for life.

Communication Form

☑ I will check what is true for me.

☐ I appreciate my life.

☐ I am grateful for certain things in my life. Some of these things are _____

____

☐ I am grateful for certain people in my life. The names of some of these people are: ______________________________________

☐ I would like to say thank you to the following people: _______________

____

☐ I would like to start a **Gratitude Journal**. It is a special book in which to write lists of things I am grateful for. Before going to bed, I may write one or more things that I or did or saw or otherwise experienced that day … things that I am grateful for.

☐ I would like to start a list of things I am grateful for, like a **Gratitude Journal,** but I would like to keep the list on a computer, instead of in a book. I could create a new document called **Gratitude Journal** on the desktop of the computer.

☐ I do not understand what it means to appreciate or to be grateful.

☐ I would like more information about this subject.

☐ I have questions or something to say about this:___________________

____

Regret

When people feel regret, they are disappointed about something they did or did not do in the past. They may feel unhappy when they think about it. They may wish that they had acted differently or made other choices. This is called "regret."

Communication Form

☑ I will check what is true for me.

☐ I feel disappointment about something in my life.

☐ I have regrets about something I did in the past.

☐ I have regrets about something I did not do. I wish I had done it.

☐ I do not have regrets.

☐ There is something that I wish I had done differently. I wish ____________

____

☐ I would like more information about this subject.

☐ I have questions or something to say about this:____________________

____

Forgiveness

To forgive means to accept that something has happened, and then to let go of the emotional pain associated with it.

People may think about their lives and choose to forgive other people for certain things that they did or said. While we forgive other people, the act of forgiving actually benefits the person who does the forgiving—by helping the forgiver let go of the emotional pain.

People may choose to forgive themselves for things that they regret.

Forgiveness is a powerful action. It requires strength of character, courage, and love.

See Chapter 18 - Quotes 8 and 9

Communication Form

☑ I will check what is true for me.

☐ I have experienced bad feelings about something or someone. The bad feelings are because ______________________________

____

☐ There are people I choose to forgive. I choose to forgive (names) _______

____

☐ There is something that I did, said, or done that I now regret. I regret that

____

☐ I choose to forgive myself for these things.

☐ I would like more information about this subject.

☐ I have questions or something to say about this:____________________

Self-Knowledge

As people grow from childhood to adolescence to adulthood, they learn more about themselves. The result of "getting to know yourself" is called "self-awareness" or "self-knowledge."

The process of gaining self-knowledge continues throughout life.

People may learn about their strengths, skills, and interests. They may learn about their challenges.

They may learn to observe how they react in different situations. They may learn to observe how they feel and what they think.

They may learn about how to improve themselves. They may learn better ways of reacting and thinking. They may learn how to communicate clearly, and how to understand others better.

They may learn to ask for help. They may learn to offer help to others.

They may learn how to live a good life. They may discover their unique purpose in life.

The process of self-knowledge continues throughout life.

See Chapter 18 – Quotes 10 and 11

Communication Form

☑ I will check what is true for me.

☐ I am learning more about myself.

☐ Some of the things I do well are ______________________________

____

☐ Some of my interests are ______________________________

____

☐ Things that are challenging to me are ______________________________

____

☐ I would like help with the following things: ______________________________

____

☐ I am able to help others with the following things: ______________________________

____

☐ I will highlight or underline sentences on the previous page that are interesting to me.

☐ I would like to learn more about myself.

☐ I would like to understand myself better.

☐ I would like other people to understand me better.

☐ I have questions or something to say: ______________________________

____

Acceptance

Acceptance is the act of receiving something. When people accept something, they receive it, or take it in.

When it has to do with an event in their lives, it means that they acknowledge that it has happened—they accept that it has happened.

Accepting ourselves the way we are is another important lesson in life.

Acceptance is often the first step to help us deal with things that cause a reaction such as feeling upset, angry, sad, or worried.

Acceptance is an intelligent and wise action.

See Chapter 18 - Quote 12

Communication Form

☑ I will check what is true for me.

☐ There is something that I need to accept. It is: ______________________

____

☐ I am not sure if there is something that I need to accept.

☐ I accept myself for who I am.

☐ I am not sure if I accept myself for who I am.

☐ I want to understand myself better.

☐ I would like more information about acceptance.

☐ I have questions or something to say about this: ______________________

____

Fear

People may fear many different things. Many people fear what they do not know. It is called "fear of the unknown."

Death is considered the "unknown"—a mystery to those of us still alive.

It is natural for many people to experience fear when going somewhere new. Dying can be compared to going somewhere new. It is natural for people to feel fear when facing death, or when they wonder about death.

However, when a person is dying, he or she may learn to look forward to what will come. With courage and trust, the fear may begin to turn into anticipation, and eventually into a peaceful feeling.

Learning that **death is a part of life** may help a person face the deaths of people and animals close to them without fear.

See Chapter 18 - Quote 13

Communication Form

☑ I will check what is true for me.

- ☐ There is something that I fear. It is: ______________________________
- ☐ I don't know if I feel fear.
- ☐ I am afraid about ____
- ☐ I would like more information about fear and how to feel trust or how to feel safe.
- ☐ I have questions or something to say: ____________________________

  ____

Courage

Courage is the quality of mind or spirit that helps a person face fear or uncertainty with confidence. Courage helps a person do what may seem too difficult or impossible to accomplish. Instead of giving up, a person can choose to have courage.

With courage, a person can accomplish more than he or she thinks. Courage is the antidote to fear.

Every person needs courage to live in the world.

It takes courage to do things that feel difficult to do.

Sometimes it takes courage to talk to other people.

It takes courage to learn about oneself, to accept some things, to learn about oneself, and to communicate.

Every person can choose to have courage in his or her life.

With courage, a person can feel confident to try new things. Choosing courage and trying what seems difficult helps a person become stronger and wiser.

Courage helps a person learn and grow to be a better person.

Communication Form

☑ I will check what is true for me.

- ☐ I understand what courage is.
- ☐ I want to understand about courage.
- ☐ Sometimes I feel afraid about ______________________________

  ____
- ☐ I would like to have courage about ______________________________

  ____
- ☐ There have been times when I have chosen to have courage.
- ☐ It took courage for me to do or say certain things. This is what I did or said that required courage: ______________________________

  ____

  ____
- ☐ If I had courage, then it would be easier for me to do or say these things:

  ____

  ____
- ☐ I have questions or something to say: ______________________________

  ____

  ____

People

Sometimes a person who is thinking about his or her life thinks about certain people.

He or she may think about the people who have been kind or helpful. He or she may think about the people who have been fun to be with. He or she may feel grateful for the people whom he or she has liked, respected, or appreciated.

A person may think about the people whom he or she loves. He or she may think about family members, friends, neighbors, teachers, co-workers, and other community members.

The person may think about people who sometimes were unkind.

The person who is facing death may want to thank certain people in his or her life. He or she may decide to forgive the people who have been unkind.

The person may think about what he or she learned from the people in his or her life.

See Chapter 18 - Quotes 14 and 15

Communication Form

☑ I will check what is true for me.

- ☐ People in my life who have sometimes been kind or helpful or fun are: (names) ______________________________

  ____

- ☐ I like to be with these people: (names) ______________________________

  ____

  ____

- ☐ There is a person or people whom I choose to thank. I want to say "thank you" to: (names) ______________________________

  ____

- ☐ Some people may have been unkind to me. Their names are: ______________________________

  ____

- ☐ There is a person or people whom I choose to forgive. I want to forgive: (names) ______________________________

  ____

- ☐ I want help thinking about the people in my life.
- ☐ I am kind or helpful to other people. If I know their names I may write them here: ______________________________
- ☐ I have been unkind to other people. If I know their names I may write them here: ______________________________
- ☐ I have questions or something to say: ______________________________

  ____

Tolerance

When people are tolerant, it means that they understand that there are many different ways of being in the world, and that is how it is supposed to be.

Tolerance is the understanding that another person's way of being commands as much respect as our own.

As they live and learn more, many people understand the importance of tolerance, instead of criticizing or judging others.

Tolerance is a practice that helps to create a peaceful society.

See Chapter 18 - Quote 16

Communication Form

☑ I will check what is true for me.

☐ I usually am tolerant of most people. I respect others even though they may be different from me.

☐ Here are names of some people whom I respect, even though they are very different from me: ______________________________

____

☐ Sometimes I do not feel tolerant of other people. Some of these people are ______________________________

☐ I would like more information about tolerance.

☐ I have questions or something to say: ______________________________

____

Respect

Respect is being polite and courteous to others.

Being respectful is a mature way to relate to others.

Children, parents, family members, teachers, friends, and others have better relationships when they respect each other.

Respect for others and for oneself helps people work, play, and live better with each other.

See Chapter 18 - Quotes 17 and 18

Communication Form

☑ I will check what is true for me.

☐ I usually try to be polite and courteous to others.

☐ I am not sure if I am polite and courteous to others.

☐ I think I am usually respectful to others.

☐ I am not sure if I am respectful to others.

☐ I try to be respectful with certain people. They are: ____________________

____

☐ I feel respected by others.

☐ I think that (names) ____________________________________ respect me.

☐ I do not feel respected by others.

☐ I think that (names) ____________________________ may not respect me.

☐ I would like more information about respect.

Kindness

Kindness is the quality of being pleasant and friendly. Kind actions are based on concern for others.

Being kind is another way for people to make daily life better for themselves and others.

An act of kindness toward another person can change a bad day into a good day—for both people. Kindness helps people feel good.

Sometimes when people are dying they may remember acts of kindness that were directed toward them in their lives.

Kindness is a gentle but powerful act.

See Chapter 18 - Quote 19

Communication Form

☑ I will check what is true for me.

- ☐ I usually try to be pleasant and friendly.
- ☐ I am not sure if I am pleasant and friendly.
- ☐ Some people are friendly to me. They are (names):__________________
- ☐ Some people are not friendly to me. If I know their names, I may write them here: ____ .
- ☐ Most people are friendly to me.
- ☐ No one is friendly to me.
- ☐ I remember a time when someone was kind to me. What this person did:

  ____

  ____
- ☐ I remember a time when I was kind to someone else. What I did: ______

  ____

  ____
- ☐ I would like more information about kindness.
- ☐ I have questions or something to say: ___________________________

  ____

Honesty

Being honest is an important trait. It means telling the truth. It means saying what is true for oneself. Good communication depends on honesty and truthfulness.

Honesty comes naturally to some people, especially many children and adults with ASD.

Honesty is an honorable trait.

The Combination of Honesty, Respect, and Kindness

Sometimes people who are honest all the time may unintentionally hurt other people's feelings.

Sometimes hearing certain types of true statements may embarrass people. Some statements about a person's appearance or other personal information may feel hurtful to the person.

People may say that their "feelings are hurt." They may feel so hurt that they may misunderstand what is being communicated. They may think that the honest person is trying to be cruel to them or is too critical.

It is often possible to be honest without hurting someone's feelings. The way to do this is to say what is true while speaking respectfully and kindly. Or learning not to say certain things is respectful and kind in some situations.

It is possible to learn to be honest, respectful, and kind at the same time. It is a communication skill.

Honesty that is tempered with kindness and respect is an honorable trait.

Communication Form

☑ I will check what is true for me.

- ☐ I usually am honest and truthful.
- ☐ I tell the truth all the time.
- ☐ Sometimes I do not tell the truth.
- ☐ I don't know if I usually am honest and truthful.
- ☐ I don't know if I have hurt someone's feelings by being honest.
- ☐ It is possible that I may have hurt someone's feelings by being honest.
- ☐ I think (name) ________________'s feelings were hurt when I said this:

  ____

  ____

- ☐ My feelings were hurt when (name)________________said something to me. What was said to me: ________________________________

  ____

  ____

- ☐ I am not sure how to be honest, respectful, and kind at the same time.
- ☐ I would like more information about how to be honest, respectful, and kind at the same time.
- ☐ I have questions or something to say:____________________________

  ____

Uncertainty

There are unexpected events in life that no one can predict. Even the most intelligent people cannot predict what is going to happen all of the time.

Life is uncertain. This means that we really cannot be sure that things will happen the way we think they will happen.

It is natural for people to have desires and preferences. It is intelligent to make plans and schedules; however, uncertainty and change are parts of life.

No one, not even teachers, parents, doctors, or others, really know for sure what is going to happen in the future. All people have to remind themselves that "change is a part of life."

Accepting that change is a part of life is an important realization that comes as people live and grow. Even though there are changes, life continues on.

Uncertainty is a part of life.

See Chapter 18 - Quote 20

Communication Form

☑ I will check what is true for me.

- ☐ I know that uncertainty and change are parts of life.
- ☐ I don't know what it means that "change is a part of life."
- ☐ I have ways to cope with uncertainty and change—and the anxiety that may result. I will check which of the following I do:
  - ☐ Use a daily schedule or daily checklist on which is written what is going to be different from usual.
  - ☐ Read information that has been written for me, explaining the change(s).
  - ☐ Reading a Social Story™ that has been written for me.
  - ☐ If I want more information about what is going to happen, ask someone to write a description and reason for the change.
  - ☐ Follow a relaxation routine, daily.
  - ☐ Go to my Quiet Area throughout the day.
  - ☐ Meditate on a regular schedule.
  - ☐ Pray on a regular schedule.
  - ☐ Exercise on a regular schedule.
  - ☐ Other: ______________________________
- ☐ I don't do most of these things, but will circle the things that I would like to try doing.
- ☐ If I show this page to a trusted person, he or she may suggest trying one or more of these things.
- ☐ I would like to learn ways to handle change and uncertainty.
- ☐ I have questions or something to say: ______________________

Faith

Faith is feeling confident that things happen the way they do for a reason. It is knowing that eventually things will be okay.

We may not know the reason why things happen the way they do, but we can try to accept and trust in the process of life. When people have faith, they are able to more easily accept what happens as they go through life, even if they don't understand why certain things happen the way they do.

People may have faith in a person. People may have faith in an idea or a belief. People may have faith in God. People may have faith in many things, or one big thing.

Having faith that there is a reason for living and dying (even if we don't always know what it is) helps people deal with the uncertainty of life.

Communication Form

☑ I will check what is true for me.

- ☐ I usually feel confident that things will be okay, eventually. I usually believe that things work out in the end.
- ☐ There are times when I am not sure if things will be okay.
- ☐ I trust certain people. The person or people whom I trust are__________

  ____
- ☐ I trust certain ideas, things or beliefs.
- ☐ I have faith in____
- ☐ I don't know what or whom I trust.
- ☐ I would like more information about faith and trust.

God

All over the world, there are people who believe in God. For those who believe, God is considered the source of all life. Some believe God to be a supernatural presence. Some believe God to be the source of true compassion and unconditional love for all life.

All over the world, there are people who do not believe in God.

All over the world, there are people who are not sure what they believe.

When people face death, they may think about God. Some people may wonder if they will be with God after they die. Some may look forward to being with God after they die. Other people may not think about God at all.

While "God" is the word commonly used by native English-speakers, different languages, cultures, religions, spiritual traditions, and individuals around the world have other names for God.

Some cultures and religions believe that there is no name for God or that God's name should not be said.

Examples of other names for "God" are:

- The Holy Trinity
- Jehovah
- Allah
- Yawheh
- I AM that I AM
- Lord of the Universe
- The One God
- The Father
- The Holy Spirit
- Christ Jesus
- True Source
- Supreme Cosmic Spirit

- Jah
- Ngal
- The Great Creator
- The Goddess
- Divine Love
- The Light
- The Great Spirit
- Life Force
- The Great Mystery
- Mother/Father God
- The Master of Life
- Shang Ti
- Lord Krishna
- The Greatest Name
- Brahman
- Absolute Love
- The Absolute
- The All
- The Alpha and Omega
- Lord
- The Creator
- The Powers of the Universe
- Other: ______________________________

See Chapter 18 - Quotes 21 and 22

Communication Form

☑ I will check what is true for me.

- ☐ I believe in God.
- ☐ I wonder if there is God.
- ☐ I don't know if I believe in God.
- ☐ I do not believe in God.
- ☐ I believe that there is a source all of life—but I am not sure what word describes my belief.
- ☐ The word or words for God that I like best from the list are ____________

  ____

  ____

- ☐ In my religion or spiritual tradition, we use the following word(s) for God: ____

  ____

- ☐ I would like more information about God.
- ☐ I have questions or something to say: ____________________

  ____

  ____

Fulfillment

Fulfillment is a kind of happiness that comes from feeling satisfied and content with life. Most people want to live a fulfilled life.

Every day we have opportunities to make choices about what we do and how we do it. When people are satisfied or happy about the choices they make and the actions they take in life, they often feel fulfilled.

For some people, fulfillment means working toward certain goals and accomplishing something.

Fulfillment may mean discovering what is true for oneself and living according to that truth.

Fulfillment may mean having good relationships with people in their lives.

Fulfillment may mean appreciating each day's experiences and being grateful for each day as it comes.

Fulfillment may mean taking pleasure in completing one thing at a time.

When people know that they did their best during their lifetime, they may feel fulfilled.

Many people feel fulfilled when they learn to accept life as it comes and appreciate each moment.

Communication Form

☑ I will check what is true for me.

☐ I am generally satisfied with my life.

☐ I am content.

☐ I know what is important to me. Important things in my life are:

____

____

☐ I want to learn more about myself and what makes me feel fulfilled.

☐ I will underline or highlight the information that I agree with on the previous page.

☐ Some of the things that are fulfilling to me are: ______________

____

____

☐ There is something that is important to me, but I have not yet accomplished or experienced it. It is: ______________

____

☐ I appreciate my life.

☐ I am not satisfied or content with my life.

☐ I want more information about fulfillment.

☐ I have questions or something to say: ______________

____

Love

People use the word "love" in many ways. There are different literal or intended meanings of the word "love."

Sometimes people say that they love a thing, like a toy or a game. Sometimes they say that they love a certain book, TV show, video, or DVD. Sometimes people say that they love doing something in particular, like playing a sport or doing art or computers. Most of these "loves" have to do with enjoying something in the physical or material world.

Sometimes people say that they love an idea or love thinking about something important to them. Sometimes people say that they love certain people. Sometimes people say that they love God.

A warm and loving feeling may be sensed by some people near the area of the physical heart. Some say that this inner, feeling heart is connected to God. This special kind of love is felt when people feel their hearts figuratively opening in a warm, big, gentle, and happy way. This heart is not the physical heart, but it is the inner feeling heart that gives, receives, and feels love.

This kind of love is described as "unconditional love" or "true compassion." This type of love stays strong even when upset, worried, sad, or angry.

"Agape" (pronounced "ah-GHA-pee") is the Greek word for this special kind of love. A Christian practice is for people to love others, even those who do not love them back.

"Loving kindness" is another way of understanding what true love is. A Buddhist practice teaches people to feel loving kindness for the Earth and all the living things of the Earth.

Teaching about love is common to many religions and spiritual traditions worldwide. Different words may be used to describe it.

It is commonly believed that if people experience "agape" and "loving kindness," then this will be good for them, for others, and for all of life.

See Chapter 18 - Quotes 23-29

Communication Form

☑ I will check what is true for me.

☐ I feel love in my life.

☐ I am not sure if I feel love in my life.

☐ I know that I am loved. I am loved by ______________________________

____

☐ I wonder if I am loved by others.

☐ I feel love for other people.

☐ I feel love for (these people, animals, and things) ____________________

____

☐ I am not sure if I feel love for other people or animals.

☐ I have questions about love and what it is.

☐ I would like more information about unconditional love, agape, and loving kindness.

☐ I have something to say or questions to ask: _________________________

____

Truth

When people face death, they often think, "**What is really true about life?**" They may wonder "**Why are we here?**" and "**What is the purpose of life?**"

Sometimes people search for truth by learning about religions, spiritual beliefs, and philosophies.

Some people search for truth by reading books, poetry, and talking with others about what they think is true about life.

Many people look for truth, day to day, while living their lives.

These are good questions to think about while living.

See Chapter 18 – Quote 30

Communication Form

☑ I will check what is true for me.

☐ I am interested in the question, **"What is really true about life?"**

☐ I have thought about this question.

☐ My ideas about this question are: ____________________________

____

☐ I am interested in the question, **"What is the purpose of life?"**

☐ I have thought about this question.

☐ My ideas about this question are: ____________________________

____

☐ I am interested in the question, **"Why are we here?"**

☐ I have thought about this question.

☐ My ideas about this question are: ____________________________

____

☐ Those questions are not interesting to me.

☐ I want to talk with, or write to (name) ____________ about these ideas.

☐ I want to learn more about those questions and related ideas.

☐ I have questions or something to say: ________________________

____

Reality

"What is reality?" is a question that people have asked throughout time.

Sometimes people consider reality to be what they can actually see with their eyes and feel with their bodies. They consider reality to be what happens to them.

There is another way of thinking about what is real. Wise people consider reality to be not what happens to us, but **how we think and feel about what happens to us.**

Thinking and feeling are powerful. What we think and how we feel about what happens to us can be considered reality because our thoughts and feelings fill our days. Our feelings and thoughts are always with us.

Cognitive Behavior Therapy is an example of a type of therapy that came from this idea. It helps people learn new or better ways to understand what happens to them.

Wise people suggest that we make our reality by what we think and how we feel about what happens to us; how we respond to experiences in our lives—the good experiences and the difficult ones.

Workbooks using Cognitive Behavior Therapy to help understand and deal with anxiety and anger are listed in Chapter 20.

Communication Form

☑ I will check what is true for me.

- ☐ I am interested in the question, **"What is reality?"**
- ☐ This question is not interesting to me.
- ☐ I want to talk with, or write to (name) ______________ about these ideas.
- ☐ I want to learn more about this question and related ideas.
- ☐ I want to learn more about how my thoughts and feelings affect the way I think about and experience my life.
- ☐ I am interested in learning about Cognitive Behavior Therapy.
- ☐ I have questions or something to say: ______________________________

____

____

What are some suggestions about how to live a good life?

Some people who have faced death give advice or suggestions about how to live a good life. A few well-respected suggestions are listed below. Information is given for each of these suggestions in this chapter.

- "Do your best."
- "Learn from your mistakes."
- "Keep a positive attitude."
- "Live life to the fullest."
- "Everyone is here for a purpose."
- "Live one day at a time."
- "Remember The Golden Rule"
- "Make the world a better place."

Communication Form

☑ I will check what is true for me.

☐ I am interested in one or more of these suggestions for living a good life. I will circle the ones that most interest me.

☐ I have something to say or questions to ask: ____________________

____

What does it mean when people say to "do your best"?

Wise people know that "doing your best" is an intelligent way to work and play. It is an intelligent way to live.

It instructs people to try to keep their attention on what they are doing, while they are doing it. It means to do things carefully. Keeping their attention on what they are doing helps people do things carefully.

Understanding the purpose of an activity or assignment can also help people do their best.

See Chapter 18 - Quotes 31 - 33

Does "doing your best" mean having to be perfect?

No, it does not mean having to be perfect. All humans make mistakes sometimes, even when they are "doing their best." No one does everything perfectly correctly all the time.

The suggestion "do your best" reminds people to work carefully and to try to keep their attention on what they are doing. A person can do his or her best, and still make mistakes. It is okay to make mistakes. Making mistakes is a necessary part of learning.

"Do your best" includes learning what to do after making a mistake.

Communication Form

☑ I will check what is true for me.

- ☐ I am interested in understanding more about what it means to "do my best."
- ☐ I have something to say or questions to ask: ______________________________

What does it mean to "learn from your mistakes"?

There are three ways of thinking about making mistakes.

1) MISTAKES ARE BAD: Some people, especially young children, think that mistakes mean that they are wrong or bad. However, it is not true that people who make mistakes are wrong or bad. **Mistakes do not mean that a person is bad.** Everyone makes mistakes sometimes. Young people make mistakes sometimes. Old people make mistakes sometimes. Intelligent people make mistakes sometimes. All human beings make mistakes sometimes.

There are better ways to think about mistakes. Here are better ways of understanding the important purpose of mistakes:

2) MISTAKES ARE MESSAGES: A better way to think about mistakes is that mistakes are messages showing people what to learn next. They may be thought of as messages from the universe, a wise person, a wizard, a master, or from God. **The message comes in the form of a mistake to get the person's attention.** It shows the person exactly what needs to be learned next. Mistakes show an intelligent person what needs to be added to his or her knowledge.

3) MISTAKES ARE CLUES: Another good way to think about mistakes is that they are clues for a detective. Detectives are happy when they find a clue. It shows them where to go or what to do next. **Mistakes are the clues for the "detective" (the person who made the mistake), showing him or her what to do next.**

SUMMARY: Mistakes are messages about what to add to a person's knowledge, or clues showing what to do next.

See Chapter 18 – Quotes 34 and 35

Communication Form

☑ I will check what is true for me.

☐ I know that everyone makes mistakes.

☐ Sometimes I think that I am the only person who makes mistakes.

☐ Sometimes I feel that I make too many mistakes.

☐ I used to think that mistakes were bad; now I know that there are good reasons for mistakes.

☐ I like the idea that **MISTAKES ARE MESSAGES.**

☐ I like the idea that **MISTAKES ARE CLUES.**

☐ I am interested in understanding more about what it means to "learn from my mistakes."

☐ I have something to say or questions to ask: ______________________________

____

What is the Seven-Step Plan to follow when a person discovers a mistake?

Here is the Seven-Step Plan to follow when a person discovers that he or she has made a mistake:

1. Stay calm. Take three slow deep breaths.

2. Think **"Okay, this is a message for me to add something to my knowledge."**

3. Think **"Okay, this is a clue showing me what to do next."**

4. Try to understand what the mistake is and fix it. OR if it cannot be fixed by yourself (if something about it is not understandable), ask someone for help. Sometimes, the best person to ask for help is the person who noticed the mistake. Or ask a trusted person for help.

5. Fix the mistake.

6. If necessary, return the work to the person who noticed the mistake.

7. Afterwards, ask yourself, "What did I learn that I am adding to my knowledge?" Think the answer to this question or tell the answer to someone close to you. "From this mistake, I learned that ____________________."

Communication Form

☑ I will check what is true for me.

☐ I am interested in using a plan to follow when mistakes are discovered.

☐ I have something to say or questions to ask: ________________________

____

What does it mean to "keep a positive attitude"?

"Attitude" refers to the way people think. Attitude affects how people act. It affects how they mature and grow. It is the energy that feeds thoughts and behavior.

A "positive" attitude is a way of thinking that is healthy and helpful.

Experiments have been done with plants to scientifically observe how a positive or negative environment affects their growth.The results of the experiments show that plants grow strong and healthy when subjected to music that creates a positive feeling. The experiments also showed that plants grow weak and sickly when subjected to music that creates negative feelings.

Doctors have noticed that people who are sick and who have a positive attitude often get well sooner than sick people who have a negative attitudes.

Laboratory research in controlled experiments using water and freezing conditions has discovered that beautiful snowflake crystals are formed when surrounded by a positive attitude. A negative attitude results in no snowflake crystals or badly-formed crystals.

A positive attitude is a healthy way of thinking. Calmly "learning from mistakes" is an example of keeping a positive attitude after making a mistake.

(Sources about these experiments are listed in Chapter 20.)

See Chapter 18 - Quote 36

Communication Form

☑ I will check what is true for me.

☐ I am interested in understanding more about "keeping a positive attitude."

☐ I have something to say or questions to ask: ____________________

Does "keeping a positive attitude" mean being happy all the time?

No, keeping a positive attitude does not mean being happy all the time. All humans experience many different emotions. Happiness is one emotion, but there are others.

A person can have a positive attitude and feel many different emotions.

It is natural for people to experience happiness, sadness, anger, frustration, fear, worry, and other emotions, at different times, on different days.

The suggestion "keep a positive attitude" reminds people to think in ways that are healthy and helpful even when feeling unhappy or anxious. Try this when feeling unhappy:

Notice the emotion that you are feeling now. Think calmly about what is happening or what is being felt, and try to understand the situation. Talk (or write) about it with someone else. Choose to believe that there is something positive to be learned from the situation.

Being willing to believe that there is something positive to be learned from the situation is an example of "keeping a positive attitude."

A person can learn to experience life, and all its "ups and downs," with a positive attitude.

See Chapter 18 – Quote 37

Communication Form

☑ I will check what is true for me.

☐ I am interested in understanding more about what it means to "keep a positive attitude."

☐ I have something to say or questions to ask: ____________________

Life is "Ups and Downs"

"Ups" are considered the things that people enjoy. "Ups" are the things that make a person feel happy or content or satisfied.

"Downs" are considered the things that make a person feel sad or angry or afraid or another uncomfortable feeling.

Life is made up of both ups and downs. Wise people say that we need to experience "downs" so we will know—and appreciate—the "ups." Opposites define one another. It would not be possible to recognize "up" without contrasting it with "down." Without both, there is neither.

Life is full of "ups and downs."

Communication Form

☑ I will check what is true for me.

☐ I am interested in understanding more about what it means that "life is ups and downs."

☐ Some of the "ups" in my life are: ______________________

____

____

☐ Some of the "downs" in my life are: ______________________

____

☐ I have something to say or questions to ask: ______________________

____

What does it mean to "live life to the fullest"?

"Doing your best," "learning from mistakes," and "keeping a positive attitude" help people "live life to the fullest."

Experiencing life, with all its "ups and downs," is another part of living life to the fullest.

Living a full life means accepting and being grateful for the ups and downs. Celebrating the "ups" and learning from the "downs" is living a full life.

Being grateful for both ups and downs is an important part of "living life to the fullest."

Living a full life requires both kinds of experiences—ups and downs.

Communication Form

☑ I will check what is true for me.

☐ I am interested in understanding more about what it means to "live life to the fullest."

☐ I have something to say or questions to ask: ______________________

____

What does it mean that "everyone is here for a purpose"?

People throughout history have wondered about the purpose of life. **"Why am I here?"** is a question that has probably been asked from ancient times. Most people wonder why they have been born and why their life is the way it is.

One answer is that each person is born into his or her life for a reason—with a particular purpose. Each person's life purpose is unique to him or her. This explains why one person is different from another person.

Each person's experiences, including mistakes and successes, are clues to his or her unique purpose. Clues may include the person's talents, skills, and interests. Clues also include difficulties or obstacles.

It has been said that "**Your greatest weakness shall be your greatest strength.**" This suggests that by accepting and learning from what is most difficult, a person may discover a hidden strength, or a personal truth, or even his or her life's purpose!

If people live their lives fully, learning from their mistakes and doing their best; they will probably fulfill their life's purpose, whatever it may be.

Someday when they are older, they may be able to describe what their life's purpose is. Or they will simply live it, with no need to talk about it.

See Chapter 18 – Quotes 38 and 39

Communication Form

☑ I will check what is true for me.

☐ I am interested in understanding more about what it means that "everyone is here for a purpose."

☐ I have something to say or questions to ask: ______________________

____

What does it mean to "live one day at a time"?

This suggests that people are to think about the present moment, with their full attention on … now. Another way to say this is to "be here now." It is also stated as "being present."

It is good to have future goals to work toward; however, it is also very important to experience the present moment, each day, and to live one day at a time.

It can be compared to walking upstairs. When walking upstairs, people must take one step at a time. Eventually they come to the top.

But on the way up, they must keep their attention on each step they take, one by one, or they may fall.

Each single step can be compared to living each single day, one day at a time. Step by step. Day by day.

The idea of "living one day at a time" is to keep our attention on what is happening right now. It reminds us to experience life in the present moment.

It means to do the best you can do, now, one step at a time.

See Chapter 18 – Quotes 40 and 41

Communication Form

☑ I will check what is true for me.

☐ I am interested in understanding more about what it means to "live one day at a time."

☐ I worry about the future. If this is true, I can try to do the following:

- Check the schedule for the day.
- Check the calendar for the week or month.
- Ask someone to help me write in the schedule or calendar the events that are coming up. Write the answers to my questions about "When will ________ happen?"
- After checking and writing on the schedule and calendar, try to remember to "be present" and do my best today, moment by moment.

☐ I sometimes worry about something specific in the future. I sometimes worry about____

____

☐ I want to learn more about "living one day at a time."

☐ I have something to say or questions to ask: ____________________

____

What is "The Golden Rule"?

Almost all philosophies and religions teach that people should treat others in a respectful and decent manner.

In North America, where this book was written, this is commonly called "The Golden Rule," from Judaism and Christianity. It is usually stated as "**Do unto others as you would wish them to do unto you.**" The same rule is found in most religious traditions and philosophies worldwide. Most people, even if they do not follow a religion, agree with "The Golden Rule."

It means that before doing or saying something to another person, first think, "**Do I want someone to say or do this to me?**" If the answer is "No," then try to remember not to do it to someone else. The idea is to treat others the way one would like to be treated.

This is understood to mean to treat others with the following qualities: respect, tolerance, kindness, and understanding. These are ways that most people want to be treated by others.

Examples of "The Golden Rule" from a variety of religious traditions and philosophies are listed in Chapter 18.

See Chapter 18 – Quotes 42 and 43

Why is it called "The Golden Rule"?

Gold is one of the most precious and valuable minerals found on Earth. The practice of treating other people the way you want to be treated "The Golden Rule" is considered a precious and valuable guideline to live by.

The practice of following this rule, "The Golden Rule," is considered precious and valuable, like gold!

Communication Form

☑ I will check what is true for me.

- ☐ Sometimes other people treat me unkindly.
- ☐ Sometimes other people treat me kindly.
- ☐ Sometimes I treat people unkindly.
- ☐ Sometimes I treat people kindly.
- ☐ I am interested in understanding more about "The Golden Rule."
- ☐ There is someone in my life whom I want to be kind to.
- ☐ I have something to say or questions to ask: ______________________

  ____

What does it mean to "make the world a better place"?

Everyone experiences difficulties—sometimes—in life.

All students and teachers, parents and children, friends and strangers, therapists and clients, supervisors and workers, have difficulties, sometimes. Everyone experiences disappointment, sadness, anger, hurt, fear, and worry sometime in his or her life.

Children and adults all over the world have severe problems such as hunger, poverty, and war.

All people experience physical and emotional difficulties sometime in their lives, no matter who they are, how old they are, how intelligent they are, or where they live.

All living things, including animals, nature, and the Earth, have problems sometimes. But there is hope.

The author's father used to tell her often as she grew up that it is important to "**leave society better than when you found it.**" Another way of saying this is to "**make the world a better place.**"

Positive change begins with one person doing one thing to make something better. Every person, young and old, can do this. Finding ways to use skills, talents, and/or interests may help make the world a better place.

It can be compared to taking the first step. And then another. And another. One step at a time.

Doing things to make the world a better place—one thing at a time—is powerful, intelligent, and compassionate.

See Chapter 18 – Quote 44 and 45

What does "a better place" mean?

The "place" refers to planet Earth. A "better place" means a better environment for people and other living things. It may mean improvements in physical health, safety and security, emotional experience, mental development, and spiritual awareness of a person or group of people. It may mean a healthier environment for all of nature, including plants, animals, and the Earth in general.

On the next few pages, ideas of how to make the world a better place are listed. Add ideas you may have.

Suggestions to improve physical health

- Learn about good nutrition.
- Avoid eating junk food, fast food, and other overly processed foods.
- Cook food in healthy ways.
- Drink clean water every day.
- Exercise alone or with others.
- Get enough sleep.
- Keep body weight within the suggested range.
- Learn about organic food, and eat it.
- Learn about locally grown food, and eat it.
- Grow a garden—organically.
- Take care of yourself when sick. (Chapters 1 & 2)
- See "Suggestions of ways to improve the environment." (page 310)
- Participate in projects to help others.
- Teach or help others to do these things.
- Other ideas: ______________________________

Suggestions to improve safety and security

- Be prepared in case of emergencies. (Chapter 1)
- Treat people considerately—no bullying.
- Report to authority figures if bullying happens. (Chapter 20)
- Report it again, and again, until bullying stops.
- Report bullying to someone else, if it doesn't stop.
- Follow safety rules at home.
- Follow safety rules at school.
- Follow safety rules while riding or driving a car.
- Follow safety rules in the community.
- Wear a safety helmet when riding a bike.
- Learn how to swim.
- Learn water safety.
- Ask for help when needed. (Chapter 5)
- Help others stay safe.
- Get to know the local police.
- Participate in projects to help others.
- Teach or help others to do these things.
- Other ideas: ______________________________

Communication Form

☑ I will underline or highlight what I am interested in.

☐ I have something to say or questions to ask: ____________________

Suggestions to improve emotional experience

- Treat others with respect and kindness. (Chapter 16)
- Treat yourself with respect and kindness. (Chapter 16)
- Report to authority figures if there is bullying. (Chapter 20)
- Report it again, and again, until bullying stops.
- Report bullying to someone else, if it doesn't stop.
- Ask for help when needed. (Chapter 5)
- Help others when they need it.
- Be a good friend.
- Learn about emotions. (Chapters 13 & 14)
- Learn ways to calm down when anxious.
- Exercise regularly.
- Make good choices of behavior.
- Use methods that make communication easier. (pen, paper, keyboard, etc.)
- Communicate with others regularly. (Chapter 5)
- Communicate what is true for you. (Chapter 5)
- Listen—to what is true for others. (Chapter 5)
- Develop tolerance and respect for others. (Chapter 16)
- Develop and use talents. (Chapters 16 &17)
- Keep a "Gratitude Journal." (Chapter 16)
- Keep a positive attitude. (Chapter 16)
- Follow "The Golden Rule." (Chapter 16)
- Participate in projects to help others.
- Teach or help others to do these things on this list.
- Other ideas: ____

Communication Form

☑ I will underline or highlight what I am interested in.

☐ I have something to say or questions to ask: ______________________

Suggestions to strengthen mental development

- Learn new information.
- Develop new skills.
- Practice skills.
- Expand talents. (Chapters 16 &17)
- Broaden interests. (Chapters 16 &17)
- Finish schoolwork.
- Finish homework.
- Solve problems in games or math.
- Do crossword puzzles, Sudoku, etc.
- Write letters, essays, articles.
- Solve real problems in life.
- Learn to follow an organizational system (checklists, schedules, labeling, etc.).
- Organize personal possessions.
- Organize school- or work-related items.
- Organize thoughts.
- Follow checklists.
- Learn from mistakes. (Chapter 16)
- Teach others to do these things.
- Other ideas: ______________________________

Communication Form

☑ I will underline or highlight what I am interested in.

☐ I have something to say or questions to ask: ______________________

____

Suggestions to improve spiritual awareness

- Do your best. (Chapter 16)
- Learn from your mistakes. (Chapter 16)
- Keep a positive attitude. (Chapter 16)
- Live life to its fullest. (Chapter 16)
- Live one day at a time. (Chapter 16)
- Follow "The Golden Rule." (Chapter 16)
- Help make the world a better place. (Chapter 16)
- Meditate.
- Pray.
- Take quiet walks in nature.
- Listen.
- Learn.
- Appreciate life. (Chapter 16)
- Be grateful. (Chapter 16)
- Appreciate beauty when you see it.
- Be kind to yourself and others. (Chapter 16)
- Communicate what is true for you. (Chapter 5)
- Listen—to what is true for others. (Chapter 5)
- Try to improve areas of your life that need improvement.
- Develop tolerance and respect for others. (Chapter 16)
- Accept yourself and others. (Chapter 16)
- Forgive yourself and others. (Chapter 16)
- Feel love for yourself, others, nature, God. (Chapter 16)
- Other ideas: ______________________________

Communication Form

☑ I will underline or highlight what I am interested in.

☐ I have something to say or questions to ask: ____________________

Suggestions to improve the environment

As this book is being written, most scientists worldwide agree that the Earth is undergoing dramatic climate changes on every continent. It is commonly referred to as "global warming."

Scientists have determined that carbon dioxide is the principal gas that is contributing to the heating up of the environment. Burning oil, gas, and especially coal, to generate electricity and heat releases carbon dioxide (CO_2) into the atmosphere.

Most of the world's production of energy is through oil, coal, and gas. People create more CO_2 each time we heat our homes, use the air conditioner, drive a car, and use an electrical appliance, including turning on the computer.

You can calculate how many tons of CO_2 you and your family produce in one year by visiting an online carbon calculator. (One site is listed at the top of the following list.) If you are a child, ask for help from your parent or other family member. You will need to enter information on your house's size, how many people live there, utility bills, and the types of vehicles. Some suggestions to help improve the environment are:

- Visit CarbonCalculator.org to calculate how many tons of CO_2 your household produces each year.
- Learn about reducing carbon dioxide emission.
- Make your home more energy-efficient.
- Conserve energy.
- Unplug electrical appliances when not in use.
- Turn off computers, TV, stereo, when not in use.
- Separate recycling from trash.
- Recycle as much as possible.
- Buy recycled products.
- Recycle computers and computer parts.
- Buy food from local farmer's markets.
- Compost kitchen waste.

- Car-pool as much as possible.
- Use public transportation.
- Where it is safe, walk or ride a bike.
- Plant trees.
- Learn about programs in your neighborhood, area, or city to improve the environment. Choose one or more to support.
- Other ideas: ____________________

See Chapter 18 – Quotes 46 and 47

Communication Form

☑ I will underline or highlight what I am interested in.

☐ I wonder how I can use my skills, talents, or interests to help make the world a better place.

☐ I have an idea of some thing(s) to do to make the world better. My idea(s) are: ____________________

☐ One thing I can do every day is ____________________

☐ One thing I can do once a week is ____________________

☐ One thing I can do once a month is____________________

☐ I do not know what to do to make the world a better place.

☐ I would like to do something to make the world a better place. I can ask (name)____________________ to help me choose something that I can do.

☐ I have something to say or questions to ask:____________________

____

What does "independent" mean?

Independent means "thinking or acting for oneself." Parents hope that their children learn how to be independent as they grow. They hope that by the time the children grow into adulthood, they will be able to take care of themselves.

Independent skills are the focus of students as they move from year to year in school.

Being independent is a common goal for most people.

Communication Form

☑ I will check what is true for me.

☐ I can do many things by myself. Some of my independent skills are: ____

____

☐ I would like to learn to be more independent with these things: ______

____

☐ I like to do some things by myself, without other people.

☐ I want to learn more about being independent.

☐ I have questions or something to say: ____________________

____

What does "*inter*dependent" mean?

Interdependent means "being responsible in relationship with others."

The idea of interdependence teaches that everyone, even the most independent people, must also rely on others in life. Interdependence is the fact that all people are a part of a family or community or workplace or, in the largest sense, the human race and all of life. We need each other.

It is okay to depend on others for certain aspects of life. Different people need others for different things. Interdependence is a fact of life that may lead to positive experiences. "Needing each other" builds community.

Independent people are usually interdependent, too. When talking about life, wise people say that "**we are all in this together.**"

Being interdependent in (and independent in some ways) is a good way to be.

Communication Form

☑ I will check what is true for me.

☐ I know that I need other people in my life.

☐ I need other people for these things:____________________________

____

☐ I like to do certain things with other people.

☐ Some things I like to do with other people are: ____________________

____

☐ Other people help me with these things: ________________________

____

☐ I sometimes help others with these things: ______________________

____

☐ I understand what it means when people say, **"We are all in this together."**

☐ I don't understand what it means when people say **"We are all in this together."**

☐ I want to learn more about interdependence.

☐ I have questions or something to say: ____________________________

____

See Chapter 18 – Quotes 48 and 49

CHAPTER 17: Being Inspired: Role Models and Mentors

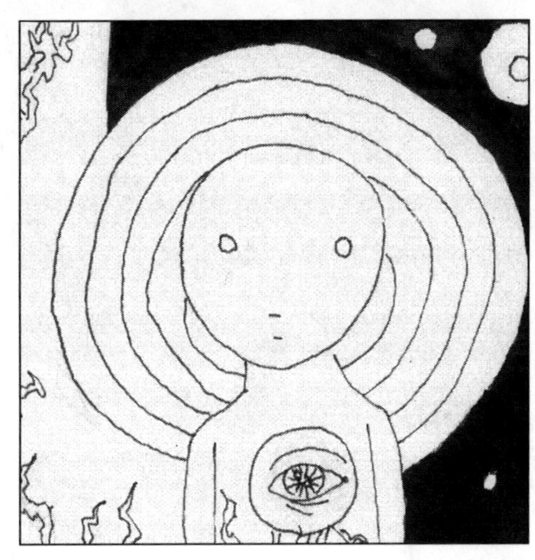

What does it mean to "be inspired"?

"Being inspired" is feeling excited and having courage and confidence.

When people are inspired they usually have a feeling of liveliness and creativity. Some people describe it as feeling "uplifted." It may be a sensation of being alert, focused, and calm at the same time.

Feeling inspired is a good feeling.

People may feel inspired about certain ideas. Sometimes people are inspired when they are learning about a certain subject. It is easy for people to feel inspired when they are using their talents and skills.

Communication Form

☑ I will check what is true for me.

- ☐ Sometimes feel inspired.
- ☐ I don't know if I have felt inspired.
- ☐ When I think about certain ideas, I feel inspired. The ideas that inspire me are ______________________________

  ____
- ☐ When I am involved in certain activities, I feel inspired. The activities that inspire me are ______________________________

  ____
- ☐ I feel inspired when I am learning about: ______________________________

  ____
- ☐ I want to feel inspired.
- ☐ I would like more information about being inspired.

Why is it important to develop skills, talents, and interests?

To develop skills and talents means to work to improve them.

Here are four good reasons for a person to develop his or her skills, talents, and interests.

1. The first reason is that the skill, talent, or interest may add pleasure and enjoyment to a person's life.

2. The second reason is that the skill, talent, or interest may lead the person to new positive experiences, which may enrich his or her life.

3. The third reason is that a person may find a job that uses his or her skills.

4. The fourth reason is that it may be a way to make the world a better place.

The following pages contain more information about these four reasons.

Reason #1: How does developing skills, talents, and interests add pleasure and enjoyment to a person's life?

It may be fun to develop a skill or talent. Becoming skilled at something may help a person feel good and enjoy life.

Learning more about one's special interest can be inspiring.

Making friends with others who have similar talent or interests can be fun.

Developing a skill, talent, or interest can add fun and enjoyment to a person's life. Sometimes it is a way to build friendships.

Communication Form

☑ I will check what is true for me.

☐ I have one or more good skills or talents. My skills or talents are:________

____

☐ I don't know if I have a skill or talent.

☐ I am very interested in the following subject(s): ____________________

____

☐ I want to improve my skills and talents, or learn more about my interest(s).

☐ I have questions or something to say: ______________________________

____

Reason #2: How may developing skills, talents, and interests lead to new positive experiences?

Using skills, talents, and interests can be like opening doors to more interests and positive experiences. Here is an example:

A young woman who lives in the United States may enjoy watching and learning about Japanese anime. Through her interest in Japanese anime, she may become curious about other aspects of Japanese culture. She may learn about Japanese food. She may go out to eat at Japanese restaurants and read Japanese cookbooks. She may learn to cook Japanese food. Her interest in cooking may grow and she may want to learn about cooking foods from other countries, as well. This interest may lead her to studying culinary arts at a community college that specializes in international cooking. This interest may also give her a context for interacting with other people by cooking special dinners to share. Perhaps this would lead to part-time work in the kitchen of a local caterer.

Developing skills, talents, and interests may help people to learn new things that lead to new positive experiences.

Communication Form

☑ I will check what is true for me.

- ☐ I may be interested in using my skills, talents, or interests in new ways.
- ☐ I would like someone to help me think of new possibilities to use my skills, talents, or interests.
- ☐ I would like to expand my skills, talents, and/or interests.
- ☐ I am not interested in expanding my skills, talents and interests.
- ☐ I am not interested now, but I may be interested sometime in the future.
- ☐ I have questions or something to say: ______________________________

Reason #3: How may developing skills, talents, and interests lead people to a job?

Skills, talents, and interests may lead adults to a job or career. In the example given in Reason #2, the young woman got a job as a result of expanding her interest in Japanese anime.

Temple Grandin and Kate Duffy have written about how skills, talents, and interests may lead to jobs in their book, *Developing Talents: Careers for Individuals with Aspergers Syndrome and High Functioning Autism.*

Communication Form

☑ I will check what is true for me.

☐ I am not old enough to have a job yet, but this idea is interesting to me.

☐ I am old enough to have a job, but I do not have one now.

☐ I have a job. It uses some of my skills, talents and or interests. On my job, the skills I use are: ________________________________

☐ I have a job and I like it most of the time.

☐ I have a job and I do not like it most of the time.

☐ I wonder what kinds of jobs may use my skills, talents, and/or interests.

☐ I would like someone to help me research the kinds of jobs that may use my skills, talents, and/or interests.

☐ I am not interested in finding out about jobs that use my skills, talents, and/or interests.

☐ Even if I do not use my special interests, skills, or talent in my job, I still enjoy using them in my hobby. My hobby (or hobbies) are: __________

____

Reason #4: How may using skills, talents, or interests make the world a better place?

Using skills and talents helps people feel inspired and "alive."

When people are inspired, they feel "full of life." Another way of saying this is that people "feel alive."

When a musician shares his or her talent by playing music, the listeners benefit when they enjoy the music. They may feel "uplifted." Sharing skills and talents may be a way to help others feel better. If more people developed and shared their skills and talents in positive ways, then more people might feel better.

Maybe the world would be a better place if there were more people feeling inspired, happy, and fulfilled.

See Chapter 18 – Quote 50

Communication Form

☑ I will check what is true for me.

- ☐ I feel more "alive" when I am involved in my skills, talents, and interests.
- ☐ I want to share my skills, talents, and interests with other people.
- ☐ I am not interested in sharing my skills, talents, and interests with other people.
- ☐ I have questions or something to say: ______________________________

  ____

What are positive role models?

Positive role models may be people who have accomplished something, or invented something, or contributed to society in other positive ways. They may be known for helping people or the environment. They may be religious figures. They may be historical figures, or have lived and died in modern times, or they may still be alive, now.

Positive role models also may be family members, community members, or other people who aren't famous, but they do their best in their lives and inspire others to do their best.

When children or teenagers or adults feel inspired by someone, they may choose to use that person as a role model. They may study the life of their role model. They may use their role model's attitude and behavior as a guide in their own lives. They may try to make choices and live and work in a similar way.

Having a role model may be a helpful, intelligent, and interesting way to be inspired to "do your best."

Can I choose a positive role model?

Yes. Any person of any age who would like to be inspired, guided, or helped in his or her life may benefit from choosing a positive role model.

A person may like to read about a famous person in history or in current times who has similar interests.

Children, teenagers, and adults may all choose to have positive role models.

Communication Form

☑ I will check what is true for me.

- ☐ I do not have a positive role model.
- ☐ I think I have a positive role model. My role model is: ______________
- ☐ I would like to have a positive role model.
- ☐ I have questions or something to say: ______________________________

____

How do people find a positive role model?

People may hear or read about how a person lived and worked. They may hear or read about the person's ideas and what he or she said and did. Reading biographies or autobiographies of role models may be interesting and inspiring.

People may choose a role model who is alive now, or who is a person from history.

The role model may be an inventor, a scientist, teacher, spiritual figure, writer, humanitarian, an artist, a musician, an athlete, a political activist, or something else.

Examples of famous role models are Abraham, Esther, Jesus, Mary (mother of Jesus), Mary Magdalene, saints, Buddha, Mohammed, Thomas Jefferson, Emily Dickenson, Thomas Edison, Marie Curie, Albert Schweitzer, Mahatma Gandhi, Albert Einstein, Henry David Thoreau, Martin Luther King Jr., Mother Theresa, Desmond Tutu, Helen Keller, Nelson Mandela, the Dalai Lama, Barbara Kingsolver, and many, many others.

People may choose a positive role model from among family members whom they admire. They may choose a role model from their grandmothers, grandfathers, mothers, fathers, step-mothers, step-fathers, aunts, uncles, godmothers, godfathers, older brothers, sisters, cousins, or others.

They may choose positive role models from among teachers, community members, or friends of the family.

People may choose one person or more than one person to be role models.

People may choose new role models as they grow older. Or they may keep the same role models for their entire lives.

Having role models may help a person be inspired to "do their best."

Communication Form

☑ I will check what is true for me.

☐ I would like to learn about a famous person or people who may be a positive role model for me.

☐ I would like help in finding out about a famous person who may be a positive role model for me.

☐ Possible famous role models for me may be (names): ________________

____

____

☐ Some positive role models from my family, school, or work may be_____

____

____

☐ Possible role models from my community may be:________________

____

____

☐ I am not interested in thinking about a role model at this time.

☐ I am not interested now, but I may be interested in finding a positive role model in the future.

☐ I have questions or something to say:________________________

____

What is a mentor?

A mentor is usually an older person—and usually someone other than a person's parents. The mentor typically enjoys the same things and has similar interests or talents as the younger person.

The mentor encourages and helps the younger person develop skills, talents, and interests. The mentor spends time with the younger person. The younger person enjoys being with and learning from the mentor. The mentor enjoys being with the younger person.

A mentor may be a family member, such as a grandmother, grandfather, aunt, uncle, or someone else.

Or a mentor may be a teacher, a parent's friend, a therapist, a neighbor, or another person in the community.

Mentors encourage the younger person to develop skills, talents, and interests. Mentors help the younger person "do his or her best."

Communication Form

☑ I will check what is true for me.

☐ I have a mentor.

☐ I do not have a mentor, at this time in my life.

☐ I am not interested in having a mentor.

☐ I would like to have a mentor.

☐ I would like someone to help me find a mentor.

☐ A mentor of mine should probably be interested in the following things:_

____

☐ I know someone in my life who may be a good mentor for me. His or her name is ______________________________________

☐ I am not interested in a mentor now, but I may be interested sometime in the future.

☐ I have questions or something to say: ______________________

____

Chapter 18: Quotes

At the beginning of the book you can read what Abraham Lincoln and Mahatma Gandhi said about life and death.

One way of learning and understanding more about life and death is by reading what has been said by people who have thought a lot about these subjects. The quotes in this chapter include fifty favorite quotes from the author's collection.

It is good to think and question and discover what is true for oneself.

Albert Einstein said this about curiosity, learning, and the mystery of life:

> *The important thing is not to stop questioning. Curiosity has its own reasons for existing. One cannot help but be in awe when he contemplates the mysteries of eternity, of life, of the marvelous structure of reality. It is enough if one tries merely to comprehend a little of this mystery every day.*
>
> *Never lose a holy curiosity.*

Quote 1

"Autism is invisible. … It is one of the things that makes me who I am … it affects the way my brain works. The brain is like a computer which is always on and keeps people living and learning.

"Autism causes my brain to sometimes work differently than other people's brains. Having a brain with autism is like having a computer with an Autism Operating System (AOS), while most other people have a Plain Operating System (POS).

"Autism is another way of thinking and being. It is not wrong or bad to have autism."

from Aspergers … What Does It Mean To Me? *by Catherine Faherty*
(AOS, POS analogy by Ellen Tanis)

Quote 2

"Those who have the strength and the love to sit with a dying patient in the silence that goes beyond words will know that this moment is neither frightening nor painful, but a peaceful cessation of the functioning of the body."

Elizabeth Kubler-Ross

Quote 3

"Death ends a life, not a relationship."

Jack Lemmon

Quote 4

"Every wise heart comes to know that life on Earth is painful as well as beautiful."

Jack Kornfield

Quote 5

"This is why we make art; it gets us through these times."

Constance Schrader

Quote 6

"It is a special gift to be able to feel things so deeply. Your feelings can soar like a kite in the wind. Listen to them and talk to them and enjoy them. But remember to protect your feelings when they might be hurt, just like you would reel in a kite when the storm comes. And if your feelings are hurt, like a kite that is torn by a strong wind, it is okay to ask for help in patching things up again. A kite can fly just as high with a patch on it … and so can you."

Dave Spicer

Quote 7

"Death can be a teacher, an advisor."

Jack Kornfield

Quote 8

"The weak can never forgive; forgiveness is an attribute of the strong."

Mahatma Gandhi

Quote 9

"Forgive your enemies."

Jesus Christ

Quote 10

"If we can keep working to gain self-awareness, then as time goes on it becomes possible to do more than merely survive. It becomes possible to take an active part in charting the course of one's life. It becomes possible to find fulfillment."

Dave Spicer

Quote 11

"I think self-awareness is probably the most important thing towards being a champion."

Billy Jean King

Quote 12

"Until you make peace with who you are, you'll never be happy with what you have."

Doris Mortman

Quote 13

"You gain strength, courage, and confidence by every experience in which you really stop to look fear in the face. You must do the thing which you think you cannot do."

Eleanor Roosevelt

Quote 14

"First of all," he said, "if you can learn a simple trick ... you'll get along a lot better with all kinds of folks. You never really understand a person until you consider things from his point of view … until you climb in his skin and walk around in it."

from To Kill A Mockingbird, *by Harper Lee*

Quote 15

"It is easy enough to be friendly to one's friends. But to befriend the one who regards himself as your enemy is the quintessence of true religion. The other is mere business."

Mahatma Gandhi

Quote 16

"Anger and intolerance are the enemies of correct understanding."

Mahatma Gandhi

Quote 17

"Respect for all life is the foundation."

The Great Law of Peace, Native American Spirituality

Quote 18

"Respect … is appreciation of the separateness of the other person, of the ways in which he or she is unique."

Annie Gottlieb

Quote 19

"If we have no peace, it is because we have forgotten we belong to one another."

Mother Teresa

Quote 20

"Everything changes, nothing remains without change."

Buddha

Quote 21

"God loves us without distinctions."

Bishop Desmond Tutu

Quote 22

"In the faces of men and women, I see God."

Walt Whitman

Quote 23

"Love (Agape) is patient, love is kind. It does not envy, it does not boast, it is not proud. It is not rude, it is not self-seeking, it is not easily angered, it keeps no record of wrongs. Love (Agape)does not delight in evil but rejoices with the truth. It always protects, always trusts, always hopes, always perseveres. Love (Agape) never fails."

from Saint Paul's first letter to the Corinthians, *the Bible*

Quote 24

"Love is the only force capable of transforming an enemy into a friend."

Rev. Martin Luther King, Jr.

Quote 25

"There is only one path to heaven. On Earth, we call it Love."

Karen Goldman

Quote 26

"Love is an endless mystery ... for it has nothing else to explain it."

Rabindranath Tagore

Quote 27

"I have never met a person whose greatest need was anything other than real, unconditional love. You can find it in a simple act of kindness toward someone who needs help. There is no mistaking love. You feel it in your heart. It is the common fiber of life, the flame that heats our soul, energizes our spirit and supplies passion to our lives. It is our connection to God and to each other."

Elizabeth Kubler-Ross

Quote 28

"Love is friendship that has caught fire. It is quiet understanding, mutual confidence, sharing and forgiving. It is loyalty through good and bad times. It settles for less than perfection and makes allowances for human weaknesses. Love is content with the present, it hopes for the future, and it does not brood over the past."

Ann Landers

Quote 29

"Compassion is not simply taking away another's pain. That may be pity—the fear of pain in ourselves and others. Compassion is the ability to allow our heart to remain open to another's suffering. There are no guidelines for this decision—just trust the heart's sense of what is right. There is really no wrong in this situation. It is just love meeting the impossible in whatever way it can."

Robert Tennyson Stevens

Quote 30

"Our life is a long and arduous quest after truth."

Mahatma Gandhi

Quote 31

"If a man is called to be a streetsweeper, he should sweep streets even as Michelangelo painted, or Beethoven played music, or Shakespeare wrote poetry. He should sweep streets so well that all the hosts of heaven and Earth will pause to say, here lived a great streetsweeper who did his job well."

Rev. Martin Luther King Jr.

Quote 32

"Act as if what you do makes a difference. It does."

William James

Quote 33

Who does his task from day to day
and meets whatever comes his way,

Believing God has willed it so,
has found real greatness here below.

Who guards his post, no matter where,
believing God must need him there,

Although but lowly toil it be,
has risen to nobility.

For great and low there's just one test,
'tis that each man shall do his best,

Who works with all the strength he can,
shall never die in debt to man.

"True Nobility" by Edgar Albert Guest
from the collection A Heap O' Livin'

Quote 34

"The person who never makes a mistake, never makes anything."

Anonymous

Quote 35

"The important thing is to learn to recover from our missteps to put things back on track."

Turk Pipkin

Quote 36

"Keep your thoughts positive, because your thoughts become your words. Keep your words positive because your words become your behaviors. Keep your behaviors positive because your behaviors become your habits. Keep your habits positive, because your habits become your values. Keep your values positive, because your values become your destiny."

Mahatma Gandhi

Quote 37

One evening an old Cherokee told his grandson about a battle that goes on inside people. He said, "My son, the battle is between two "wolves" inside us all.

One is Evil. It is anger, envy, jealousy, sorrow, regret, greed, arrogance, self-pity, guilt, resentment, inferiority, lies, false pride, superiority, and ego.

The other is Good. It is joy, peace, love, hope, serenity, humility, kindness, benevolence, empathy, generosity, truth, compassion, and faith.

The grandson thought about it for a minute and then asked his grandfather, "Which wolf wins?"

The old Cherokee simply replied, "The one you feed."

Anonymous

Quote 38

"If we are to achieve a richer culture…we must recognize the whole gamut of human potentialities, and so weave a less arbitrary social fabric, one in which each diverse gift will find a fitting place."

Margaret Mead

Quote 39

"Being alive is itself an expression of mystery. The clues to our inner nature are always around us."

Jack Kornfield

Quote 40

"Satisfaction lies in the effort, not in the attainment of a goal. Full effort is full victory."

Mahatma Gandhi

Quote 41

"The great composer . . . does not set to work because he is inspired. He becomes inspired because he is working. Beethoven, Wagner, Bach, and Mozart settled down day after day to the job in hand with as much regularity as an accountant settles down each day to his figures. They didn't waste time waiting for inspiration."

Ernest Newman

Quote 42

"Every religion emphasizes human improvement, love, respect for others, sharing other people's suffering. On these lines every religion had more or less the same viewpoint and the same goal."

The Dalai Lama

Quotes 43

Socrates: "Do not do to others that which would anger you if others did it to you."

Greece; 5th century BC

Native American Spirituality: "All things are our relatives; what we do to everything, we do to ourselves. All is really One."

Black Elk

Hinduism: "This is the sum of duty: do not do to others what would cause pain if done to you."

Mahabharata 5:1517

Buddhism: "... a state that is not pleasing or delightful to me, how could I inflict that upon another?"

Samyutta NIkaya v. 353

Judaism & Christianity: "... thou shalt love thy neighbor as thyself."

Leviticus 19:18

Islam: "None of you [truly] believes until he wishes for his brother what he wishes for himself."

Number 13 of Imam "Al-Nawawi's Forty Hadiths."

Confucianism: "Do not do to others what you do not want them to do to you."

Analects 15:23

Quote 44

"Although the world is full of suffering, it is also full of the overcoming of it."

Helen Keller

Quote 45

"You don't have to see the whole staircase, just take the first step."

Rev. Martin Luther King Jr.

Quote 46

"We know that the air we breathe is shared with the oaks and fir trees of the forests, that the water we drink pours down from floating clouds as rain before it comes into our cells ... we discover that we have the same last name as the mountains, the streams, and the redwood trees."

from After the Ecstasy, the Laundry, *by Jack Kornfield*

Quote 47

"To laugh often and much; to win the respect of intelligent people and the affection of children; to earn the appreciation of honest criticism and endure the betrayal of false friends; to appreciate beauty and find the best in others; to leave the world a bit better, whether by a healthy child, a garden patch, a redeemed social situation; to know even one life has breathed easier because you have lived—that is to have succeeded."

Ralph Waldo Emerson

Quote 48

"Interdependence is and ought to be as much the ideal of man as self-sufficiency. Man is a social being. Without interrelation with society he cannot realize his oneness with the universe or suppress his egotism."

Mahatma Gandhi

Quote 49

"And the King shall answer and say unto them, Verily I say unto you, Inasmuch as ye have done unto one of the least of these my brethren, ye have done unto me."

Jesus Christ, from the Bible, Matthew 25:40

Quote 50

"Do not ask what the world needs. Instead ask what makes you come alive. Because what the world needs is more people who have come alive."

Thurmond Whitman

CHAPTER 19: Just for Fun: Idioms

What are some idioms and expressions using the word "dead" that do not literally mean it?

The following pages list twenty examples of idioms and expressions in the English language, with their intended meanings.

Even though each expression includes the word "dead" or "die," it does not literally mean those words, as defined elsewhere in this book. It may be fun to ask family members, friends, teachers, and others to try to give examples of these expressions by using them in sentences. It may also be fun to come up with sentences together, using some of these expressions.

You can find a collection of over 2,000 English idioms and expressions with their definitions, on the website: www.usingenglish.com/reference/idioms.

Deadbeat

Someone who is useless or a failure at something.

Deadline

The designated date when a project or assignment is supposed to be finished.

Dead as a dodo

To be totally hopeless, with no chance of success. Dodo birds have been extinct for a long time.

Dead as a doornail

Same as above.

Dead bolt

A type of door lock that is very secure; cannot be broken.

Dead duck

A person or project unlikely to continue or survive; is ruined.

Dead end

A road or street that ends; is not connected to another road.

Dead Head

A fan of the rock band, "Grateful Dead" so much that he or she went to many concerts, and/or followed them on tour, and/or now listens to their music regularly.

Dead heat

A race or game that is being played and/or ends in a perfect tie. The participants showed equal ability.

Do or die
To succeed completely, or fail completely; to risk total failure while trying to succeed.

Dead pan
An expressionless face and monotone voice while telling a joke or saying something that is funny.

Dead tired
To be very tired; exhausted.

Dead to the world
To have fallen into a deep sleep; extremely difficult to wake up.

Beat a dead horse
To continue fighting for something which has been lost; to keep arguing a point which has already been decided.

I'm dying to tell you...
To have a very strong desire to tell you something.

It's almost dead
When an electrical appliance or battery is very low on electrical energy.

It's dead
When an electrical appliance or battery is totally out of electrical energy.

Let it die
To give up on an idea or desire; to stop thinking about it.

That's to die for

To like or enjoy an item or a particular food very much; to have an extremely strong desire for it.

Death by Chocolate

A popular name for a dessert containing mostly chocolate ingredients. It may be a cake, pie, pastry, or pudding.

CHAPTER 20: Resources for More Information

Primarily for Adults

Gone From My Sight: The Dying Experience
by Barbara Karnes, RN.

A Hospice nurse wrote this simple fourteen-page booklet. It provides concrete information about the physiological changes during the last few weeks, days, and hours, of the person who is dying.

Bedridden during his last months, my dad became agitated and uncomfortable with his body's physical symptoms, asking me repeatedly **"Why do I feel like this?"** I would take a deep breath and softly answer that I thought it was because he was dying and he was feeling the symptoms of his body shutting down.

My dad valued education and learning about things that were new to him. I felt it was important for him to become familiar with the roadmap, to be educated about the amazing transition he was experiencing, as he died a natural and peaceful death at home.

Although the Hospice social worker emphasized that this booklet ***Gone From My Sight*** was meant to be read by my mother, brother, and me, I gave it to my dad to read.

I remember that day he read it over and over, between increasingly long periods of sleep. He became calmer and his anxiety clearly decreased. One time he looked up at me with eyes full of concern and compassion and handed me the booklet and said, *"I want you to read this book."*

Three days later he fell peacefully into his last sleep.

Gone From My Sight does not use spiritual or religious terms, although its pragmatic honesty and clarity about the physical changes, its affirmation that dying is ultimately a solitary journey, and its poetic suggestion that the person is beginning something new feels to me like holy scripture. I believe it served my father in that way.

Gone From My Sight can be ordered through Barbara Karnes Books, P.O. Box 822139, Vancouver, WA 98682, or obtained through your local Hospice.

"forever hold your penguin dear"
Patti Digh

This essay located on Patti's award-winning blog, ***37days*** (**37days.typepad.com**), **"forever hold your penguin dear"** is a compassionate and eloquent account of how my friends and family responded to the death from a automobile accident of Meta Bowers-Racine on September 14, 2006. Meta is mentioned several times in this book: in the Dedication; in the Message From The Author; in Meet The Illustrator, and in the Acknowledgments.

It was two weeks after the experience chronicled in the essay **"forever hold your penguin dear,"** that I started writing this book.

"Stages of Grief In Children"
Susan Moore, M.A.

This short article gives clear guidelines and supports understanding the process of grieving in children and suggestions about how to support them. The stages are defined as denial (shock, numbness); acute grief (sadness, depression, anger, guilt, anxiety, fears, regression, physical distress) and adjustment (painful acceptance of reality, reestablishment of life). This article can be found on the web at **Californiasids.com.**

On Grief and Grieving
Elizabeth Kubler-Ross and David Kessler

This is the last of eighteen books written by Dr. Kubler-Ross, right before she died in 2005. Dr. Kubler-Ross was the foremost pioneer of the compassionate death-and-dying movement, educating the medical establishment and the public on a large scale. Below is an excerpt from the concluding pages 229 - 231 of Kubler-Ross and Kessler's book:

> "Why grieve? For two reasons. First, those who grieve well, live well. Second, and most important, grief is the healing process of the heart, soul, and mind; it is the path that returns us to wholeness … It doesn't mean we forget; it doesn't mean we are not revisited by the pain of loss. It does mean we have experienced life to its fullest, complete with the cycle of birth and death."

"The Agreement"
Catherine Faherty

I wrote this essay a few weeks following the death of my father. It tells the story of our agreement that he fulfilled after he died. "The Agreement" can be found in the December 2005 issue of Western North Carolina Woman, Volume 4, Number 12. To read this essay online, go to **http://wnc-woman.com/1205-the_agreement.html**

Hospice
hospicenet.org

This comprehensive program of care to patients and families facing a life-threatening illness is available in most areas of the country (USA) and internationally. Hospice affirms life and regards dying as a normal process. It neither hastens nor postpones death. The dying and their families are comforted. Hospice provides personalized services and a caring community so that people can prepare for death in a way that is most meaningful to them. The patient and family are both included in the care plan. Emotional, spiritual and practical support is given based on personal needs and wishes.

Five Wishes
www.agingwithdignity.org

This booklet was made to be completed by any individual 18 or older, stating how he or she requests to be treated in the event of a serious illness. It is a living will that talks about personal, emotional and spiritual needs, as well as medical wishes. It lets the person choose who is to make health care decisions if he or she is not able to make them. It was written with the help of ***The American Bar Association's Commision on the Legal Problems of the Elderly,*** and leading experts in end-of-life care. It is easy to use, requiring the person to check boxes, circle directions, or write a few sentences. It has been described by Time magazine and Money magazine as "the first living will with a heart." ***Five Wishes*** is available in twenty languages.

Animal Hospice
pethospice.org

A new kind of animal care based on human hospice is Nikki Hospice Foundation for Pets in Vallejo, CA. Pet lovers can care for their dying animals at home under the guidance and assistance of hospice veterinarians and a professional, qualified staff. Developed as an alternative to traditional veterinary medicine which traditionally offers dying animals aggressive treatments, followed by euthanasia—is the nation's first and currently only nonprofit organization devoted to the provision of home hospice care for terminally ill companion animals.

Donate Life America
donatelife.net

This not-for-profit alliance of national organizations and local coalitions across the United States is dedicated to inspiring all people to save and enhance lives through organ, eye and tissue donation.

Nobelity
Turk Pipkin

A stunning look at the world's most pressing problems through the eyes of nine Nobel Laureates, ***Nobelity*** is a film that follows the filmmaker's personal journey to find enlightening answers about the kind of world our children and grandchildren will know. Filmed in U.S., France, England, India, and Africa, Nobelity combines the insights of nine distinguished Nobel Peace Prize winners with a first-person view of world problems and the children who are most challenged by them. To order a DVD, go to **www.nobelity.com**

ONENESS: Great Principles Shared by all Religions
Jeffrey Moses

This book is described as the collected wisdom of the world's religions showing the "oneness" of the human spirit. This book contains commentaries and scriptural selections for sixty-five principles showing how they are expressed in the world's major religions. For more information, visit **onenessonline.com.**

After the Ecstasy, the Laundry: How the Heart Grows Wise on the Spiritual Path
Jack Kornfield

Drawing on the experiences and insights of leaders and practitioners within the Buddhist, Christian, Jewish, Hindu, and Sufi traditions, this book shows how the modern spiritual journey unfolds while preparing the heart for awakening. Family relationships, emotional pain, work, sickness, loss, and death are some of the topics covered through personal stories and traditional tales.

TEACCH
Treatment and Education of Autistic and Communication Handicapped Children/Adults
TEACCH.com

The University of North Carolina at Chapel Hill's School of Psychiatry has been the home of the **TEACCH** Program since the early 1970s. Founded by the late Eric Schopler, and directed by Gary Mesibov, the **TEACCH** approach includes a focus on the person with autism and the development of a program around his or her skills, interests, and needs. The major priorities include centering on the individual, understanding autism, adopting appropriate adaptations, and a broadly-based intervention strategy building on skills and interests. By focusing on the individual we mean that the **person is the priority**, rather than any philosophical notion such as inclusion, discrete trial training, facilitated communication, etc. **TEACCH** emphasizes individualized assessment to understand the individual and to acknowledge and better understand "the culture of autism," suggesting that people with autism are part of a distinctive group with common characteristics that are different, not inferior to others.

The Gray Center for Social Learning and Understanding
TheGrayCenter.org

The Gray Center is an organization dedicated to individuals with autism spectrum disorders and those who work alongside them to improve mutual understanding. The social impairment in ASD is approached as a shared impairment. Social understanding strategies such as Social Stories™ and Comic Strip Conversations were developed to improve social understanding on both sides of the social equation. The clear, literal, and reassuring writing style of this book, ***Understanding Death and Illness***, is characteristic of Social Stories.

Developing Talents: Careers for Individuals with Asperger's Syndrome and High Functioning Autism
Temple Grandin and Kate Duffy

This book was mentioned in **Chapter 17**. It covers relevant aspects of the search for careers for individuals on the autism spectrum, with a large collection of possible careers.

"Up A Creek Without An Idiom"
Tori Gallagher

This essay was written by a mom of two sons with Aspergers. I was prompted to include this essay as a resource when I was working on **Chapter 19**. This highly recommended essay can be found in the **May-June 2006 issue of the *Autism Asperger Digest Magazine,*** published by Future Horizons. (If you are a teacher or parent, or just anyone who appreciates the fresh uniqueness of an Asperger's point of view, you really need to read about George's and Tori's adventures with idioms!) More of Tori Gallagher's insightful, sometimes irreverent, always honest and deeply touching essays can be found in several issues of the *Autism Asperger Digest.* Visit **www.autismdigest.com**

For Both Children and Adults

Lost and Found: A Kid's Book For Living Through Loss
Rabbi Marc Gellman and Monsignor Thomas Hartman

Full of reader-friendly advice for coping with "losing stuff" like losing a game, losing a friend, losing a parent in a divorce, losing confidence, losing trust, losing a loved one, and more; this book helps the readers look past their loss with hope instead of pain and anger. **I especially recommend pages 124-135 (The Way Death Comes) from the book, *Lost and Found*, which clearly and compassionately describes four different experiences of dying: sudden death, slow death, painful death, and peaceful death.**

Aspergers ... What Does It Mean To Me?
Catherine Faherty

The first half of each chapter of ***Aspergers ... What Does It Mean To Me?*** consists of workbook pages for the child or youth with high functioning autism or Aspergers. The highly structured workbook pages provide information about different aspects of daily life—while they discover and express their thoughts, questions, ideas, and personality traits. The second part of each chapter is for parents, teachers, and other adults, providing an abundance of practical strategies to support their child's development. TEACCH Structured Teaching strategies are featured within many of the chapters. The twelve chapters include topics such as: Ways of Thinking, The Sensory Experience, Artistic Talent, People, Understanding, Thoughts, Communication, School, Friends, and Feeling Upset.

DoveSong.com

This website is a public educational service dedicated to providing information about the great music traditions of the world—classical and folk music that touches the spirit. Created by composer Ron Robertson and Mary Ellen Bickford, DoveSong.com's purpose is to acquaint and educate people worldwide with the concept of "positive music." Positive music describes the effect of musical sound, not the lyrical content or the message of a song (a common use of the term today). Just as pure natural foods and fresh air help contribute to a healthy body, music that is pure and inspired contributes to healthy emotions and spirit. **This website provides information and links to the body of scientific research related to plant health referred to in Chapter 16 under the topic of keeping a positive attitude.**

The Secret of Water
Masaru Emoto

Introducing children to the wondrous world of water, this book shows why treating this precious resource with respect is so vital to our personal health and the well-being of the planet. Entertaining and educational for both adults and children alike, **this book refers to the results of scientific research into water crystal formation that was mentioned in Chapter 16 under the topic of keeping a positive attitude.**

Try and Stick With It
Cheri Meiners

It's hard to try new things—for adults as well as children. It's even harder to stay the course when something is more difficult than we thought it would be, or when things don't work out the way we had hoped. Yet flexibility and perseverance are essential to success in all areas of life, at all ages. This book introduces children to the benefits of trying something new and the basics of stick-to-it-iveness. Includes suggestions adults can use to reinforce the ideas and skills being taught. Check out the entire series of books by Cheri Meiners, including these additional titles: ***Accept and Value Each Person; Be Careful and Stay Safe; Be Polite and Kind; Join In and Play; Know and Follow Rules; Listen and Learn; Reach Out and Give; Respect and Take Care of Things; Share and Take Turns; Talk and Work It Out;*** **and** ***Understand and Care.***

No Fishing Allowed
Carol Gray and Judy Williams

Statistics show that most children on the autism spectrum have been targets of bullying attempts. *No Fishing Allowed* is a violence-prevention program for elementary school students to teach them and their teachers how to prevent bullying. It gives teachers and students the tools to create safe schools through organized efforts to establish an accepting and friendly learning environment for all students. It addresses peer conflict vs. bullying, and tattling vs. reporting. It covers different types of bullying: friendship bullying, and gender-specific bullying, and emphasizes empowerment strategies.

Exploring Feelings: Cognitive Behaviour Therapy to Manage Anxiety* and *Exploring Feelings: Cognitive Behaviour Therapy to Manage Anger
Tony Attwood

The programs in these two workbooks are designed to explore and manage anger and anxiety. They help the child understand the mental world from a scientific perspective—using the metaphor of the child being an astronaut or scientist exploring a new planet. These highly structured workbooks include activities and information related to the feelings of being happy, relaxed, anxious or angry. Individual comments and responses are meant to be recorded in these workbooks.

Wikipedia
wikipedia.org

This online encyclopedia provides easy access to definitions and information, especially motivating for those who like to work and play on the computer.

A Prose-Poem

by John Engle

I've heard it said that we come into this world with nothing and we go out of it with nothing. In a sense this is true, in a sense not, and in a sense it's backwards. This last aspect is clearer when I visualize life in reverse. Many years ago, as an old man, I wandered off to a lovely meadow and died.

Now, several years post-mortem, I turn and go back. On the spot where I died, my bones have relaxed and become lodged, to varying degrees, in the soil all around. Critters have made-off with a few, but they will bring them back now. The soil is rich, as many others, before and since, have died in this meadow, some on this spot. As I near my death-birth, water flowing in reverse brings my bones closer; their richness in the soil concentrates beneath them.

All my bones are back, and like waves, generations of fungi and bacteria sacrifice their biomass to my growing corpse-fetus. In appearance, this collection of richness is becoming humanoid; more-so as carrion eaters, mostly crows and insects, vomit their contributions. Until finally, with all things borrowed returned, I am a finished corpse, and life is a breath away. Like a flame which, lighting a candle, remains undiminished, the Earth grants life to forms. Can my heart hear? Yes, because I have ears. Is the Earth alive? Yes, because it creatures.

The last-first beat of my heart is so weak, my last-first breath so shallow. My eyes remain closed for a time as my strength fades back. Finally I am vibrating, coursing, humming with activity. There is nothing left but to become aware. I open my eyes. I am still covered by twigs, leaves, and other relics of the womb. They fall away as I sit up.

Where did I come from? I am an old man, full of knowledge, but not answers. I am also very new, and have not yet lost my capacity to observe without judgment. I did not come into this world, I came out of it. Where am I going? As I grow younger I will forget so much until, at the very beginning-end, I will be nothing but a hum of pure life, absorbed back into the life and body of my mother. I do not go out of this world, I go into it, when all things borrowed are returned.

The One True Freedom

by William Sloane Coffin

The one true freedom in life is to come to terms with death, and as early as possible, for death is an event that embraces all our lives.

And the only way to have a good death is to lead a good life.

Lead a good one, full of curiosity, generosity, and compassion, and there's no need at the close of the day to rage against the dying of the light. We can go gentle into that good night.

Acknowledgments

Thank you to Suzie Heaton for sending me her essay "Where is Mr. Paul?" as soon as she heard I was writing this book. Thank you to John Engle for permission to include his prose-poem, his astute editing assistance, friendship, and his constant presence on our panels of adults with ASD. Thank you to Nancy MacDonald for telling me the tender and powerful story about her son Isaac and his grandmother (page 18). Thank you to Thomas Johnson for his exquisite and intuitive illustrations; to Gary Mesibov for writing the Foreword; and to Kelly Gilpin at Future Horizons for her support, enthusiasm, patience, and graciousness. Thank you to my cousin Irene Vassos for her unconditional love, manifesting itself this time as assistance with the book layout; and her, Alice Cruickshank's, and Claire's welcoming writing corner. Thank you to Ginger Graziano for her timely willingness with technical support, skill, warmth, and reassurance exactly when I needed it. Gratitude to the Greek and Turkish music of Asia Minor played by Muammer Ketencoglu which accompanied me during the creation of this book—I heard my late grandparents calling to me through his accordion.

My support team was led by my first teacher-of-the-power-of-creativity-all-things-are-possible mother Ismene Collins; my rock-steady pillar, spotter, and beloved partner in life John Faherty; my heart—my talented, inspiring, and visionary son Nicholas Faherty (who suggested I include a chapter on idioms); my favorite aunt Jane Maxouris; and my awesome cousin-sister Irene Vassos. My grandson Kai Faherty filled me with joy and delight, along with his mother Shawn Duff's reassuring mantra that "it'll be okay," even when I was tired and grieving. And always forever thank you to my cornerstones, Odette Petrini, Sheila O'Brien, Mary Anne Bowers, and Deb Criss.

Moreover, I am deeply grateful for those whose support and checking in with me at the perfect time during the birthing of this book was more helpful than they know. Thank you! They include Boone, Claudia, Papa Michael, Raven, Patti, John, Lillah, Janna, Stuart, Laurie, Maria, Janis, Joseph, Dayna, Jodi, Tommy, Sue, Ron, Linda, Bari, and Jeff. And to Raj, whom I think about daily with love. I appreciate and thank my colleagues at the Asheville TEACCH Center for their patience and support—Steve Love, Pat Greene, Margie Catalano, Chris Reagan, Stephanie Troop, Galene Fraley, Anne McGuire, Viviana Saraceno, Jon Blalock, and Carolyn Ogburn, (who promised me that she would finish this book if I could not). Thank you to my compatriots in Greece who are waiting for this book; Christos Alexiou, Vaya Papageorgiou, and Margarita Gogaki.

I bow down again, in awe and gratitude to Mary Anne Bowers—cowgirl, neighbor, beloved friend-sister, and half-mother. From Mary Anne I learn about kindness, faith, goodwill, adventure, loyalty, strength, surrender, and especially about love. I pray that I can emulate even a small bit of Mary Anne's grace (and her's and Raj's ukelele chords). I try to remember that we all are on the path toward our day of passage, every day, whether or not we have a medical diagnosis of a terminal illness. And today, here and now, is what our life on Earth is made of. We have this minute, now.

And finally, thank you for the inspiration I've received from those who have passed on, especially my father Nicholas Collins; and Uncle George Kollias, *Yiayia* Katina Kollias, *Yiayia* Katina Maxouris, Dorothy Faherty, Paul Faherty, Auntie Day Vassos, Uncle Nick Vassos, Grace Mona Levin, Helena Stevens, Bessie Parks, Eric Schopler, Margaret Lansing, Sara Handlan, Andrew Longcoy, Minas Vassos, and our Ambassador of Love, Meta Bowers-Racine.

The Illustrator

Thomas Johnson was drawing before he could walk or talk, and was diagnosed with autism when he was three. At age ten, he drew over seventy charming illustrations found in Catherine Faherty's best-selling book ***Aspergers ... What Does It Mean To Me?***

While Thomas is open to a wide variety of visual media, his chief influences in illustration have been Maurice Sendak, Arthur Rackham, Kay Neilson, Aubrey Beardsley and Wanda Gag. A 2007 graduate of Asheville High School in Asheville, North Carolina, Thomas currently attends the University of the Arts in Philadelphia, Pennsylvania, where he is majoring in film. He would also like to pursue a career writing and illustrating children's books. Thomas is honored to be part of this book, and hopes he was able to interpret the material through illustration in an honest and sensitive way.

Thomas dedicates the collection of the seventeen pen and ink llustrations in this book to the memory of his father, Eugene Walter Johnson; his grandmother, Pauline Anna Ponder Harrison; and friends, Meta Bowers-Racine and Andrew Longcoy.

The Author

Photograph by Marilyn Ferikes

At age thirteen, when volunteering at a summer day camp for children with special needs near Chicago, Catherine knew immediately that this would be her life's work. Her early education and training in the mid 1970s was at Eastern Michigan University in Ypsilanti, Michigan, where she worked each afternoon after her classes at the lab school for exceptional children on campus. Since 1985 she has been affiliated with the TEACCH Program, first as a classroom teacher and later as a psychoeducational specialist at the Asheville TEACCH Center, one of North Carolina's nine regional TEACCH Centers through the University of North Carolina at Chapel Hill. Numerous activities fill her days at the TEACCH Center; weekly diagnostic evaluations for children and adults; educational sessions for parents, children, and adults with ASD; social groups for adults with autism; support groups for parents; and consulting to school systems. Catherine is a Lead Teacher and Trainer for TEACCH trainings nationally and internationally; she helped create and develop several training models, wrote the manual, ***TEACCH Structured Teaching Assessment: Guides to Individualizing the Schedule and Work System***, and the book ***Aspergers … What Does It Mean To Me?*** Published in 2000 by Future Horizons, it was the first book of its kind written for children and youth with ASD to help them understand what it means. Translated into several languages, including Greek, Swedish, Spanish, Japanese, French, Norwegien, and Danish, this reader-friendly book features activities to help build self-awareness and self-esteem for verbal children with ASD, along with a wealth of Structured Teaching strategies for their parents and teachers. One of the few world-wide authorized trainers of Social Stories™, Catherine Faherty also enjoys promoting and teaching Social Stories™, as introduced and taught by Carol Gray and **The Gray Center for Social Understanding.**

Catherine's father emigrated to the United States from southern Greece, and her maternal grandparents emigrated from Asia Minor—from the current Aegean coastal cities of Izmir and Alacati, Turkey. Her Greek heritage is an important part of her personal and professional life. Catherine has supported the The Greek Society for the Protection of People with Autism since 1995 when she first met its visionary founder, Professor Christos Alexiou in Athens, Greece. Founding The Greek Autism Project of Asheville, NC, together with the Asheville Daughters of Penelope and AHEPA Chapters (American Hellenic Educational Progressive Association), she spearheaded fund-raising efforts to purchase educational and assessment instruments for therapists in Greece, and to fund the translation of books on autism into the Greek language.

Catherine Faherty enthusiastically offers this new book, ***Understanding Death and Illness and What They Teach About Life***, to the autism spectrum community and its support circles—families, friends, professionals, and others.